# A Look at

# Moons

Ray Spangenburg and Kit Moser

Franklin Watts

A DIVISION OF GROLIER PUBLISHING
NEW YORK • LONDON • HONG KONG • SYDNEY
DANBURY, CONNECTICUT

*In memory of*
ROBERT L. DURHAM
*(1912–1998), a builder of dreams*

Photographs ©:Art Resource, NY: 14 (Scala); Astron Society of the Pacific: 58; Corbis-Bettmann: 55; Finley Holiday Films: 61 left, 40 (NASA), 50; Liaison Agency, Inc.: cover center (NASA-JPL); NASA: cover top right, cover top left, cover bottom, 6, 9, 17, 18, 20, 21, 35, 39, 53, 60, 61 right, 70, 71, 72, 73, 79, 83, 84, 95, 106, 109, 110; National Museum of Natural History, Smithsonian Institution: 13; North Wind Picture Archives: 74; Photo Researchers: 57, 96 (Chris Buttler/SPL), 54 (David Ducros/SPL), 30, 31, 44, 45 (NASA/SPL), 12 (Rev. Ronald Royer/SPL), 28, 29, 64, 65, 86, 87, 99, 103 (SPL); Photri: 32, 42, 46, 49, 62, 100, 104; Royal Observatory Edinburgh: 25 (D. Malin).

**Visit Franklin Watts on the Internet at:**
**http://publishing.grolier.com**

Library of Congress Cataloging-in-Publication Data

Spangenburg, Ray.
    A look at moons / by Ray Spangenburg and Kit Moser.
        p.    cm.—(Out of this world)
    Includes bibliographical references and index.
    Summary: Describes the physical characteristics of the moons in our solar system and the processes and spacecraft used to gather information about them.
    ISBN 0-531-11702-2 (lib. bdg.)        0-531-16514-0 (pbk.)
    1. Satellites—Juvenile literature. [1. Satellites. 2. Solar system. 3. Outer space—Exploration.] I. Moser, Diane, 1944– II. Title. III. Series: Out of this world (Franklin Watts)
QB401.5.S64    2000
523.4—dc21
                                    99-15452
                                          CIP

GROLIER
PUBLISHING

# Acknowledgments

A book involves a lot more than a couple of writers sitting down at a computer keyboard and hammering out sentences. The knowledge, expertise, and resources of many people flow into the mix, and we would especially like to thank some of the many people who have contributed to *A Look at Moons*.

First of all, a special appreciation to Sam Storch, lecturer at the American Museum-Hayden Planetarium, who reviewed the manuscript and made many excellent suggestions. Also a special thanks goes to our editor at Franklin Watts, Melissa Stewart, whose steady flow of enthusiasm, creativity, energy, and clippings of late-breaking news have infused this series.

For past conversations, thanks to Torrence Johnson, project scientist for the Galileo Mission, and to Christopher P. McKay, exobiologist and planetary scientist at the National Aeronautics and Space Administration (NASA) Ames Research Center. Finally, to Tony Reichhardt and John Rhea, once our editors at the old *Space World Magazine*, thanks for starting us out on the fascinating journey we have taken during our years of writing about space.

# Contents

*Viking 2* recorded this color-enchanced image of Phobos, one of Mars moons, on September 18, 1976.

# Chapter 1

# Worlds Around Worlds

Scientists used to think of our solar system as a quiet corner of the Universe where nine planets calmly orbited a warm, kind Sun. Between 1971 and 1989, humans sent several spacecraft to explore our closest neighbors. As the Viking spacecraft flew by Mars, it tantalized us with stunning views of the planet and its moons. A few years later, *Voyager 1* and *Voyager 2* traveled to the outer solar system. They gave us our first good look at the moons and planets that reside there. The images supplied by these early spacecraft showed us that the planets and their moons are much more active and violent than we had ever imagined.

Since that time, we have learned that our solar system includes more than just the Sun, nine planets, and a few moons. We have seen and studied many new worlds. We have discovered that some of the moons orbiting the outer planets are larger than Pluto and Mercury. We have also found that three moons in the solar system may have supported life forms at one time or another. Could life still exist on another world within our solar system? Even if the answer is "no," it is now clear that the moons are among the most exciting and important objects in the solar system. The variety and exotic fascination of these celestial bodies seems unlimited.

## Why Look at Moons?

For thousands of years, people looked up at the night sky and wondered about the big, pale disk they saw there. It seemed to grow and shrink as the days passed. Sometimes it looked as if a giant bite had been taken out of it. Sometimes it hovered on the horizon, looking like a huge, golden plate. People saw—or thought they saw—relationships between the Moon's phases and the events in their lives.

Ancient peoples asked many questions about the Moon. They wondered what it was made of. They wanted to know if other creatures lived there and, if so, what they were like. Most importantly, they wondered whether humans could travel there.

By the twentieth century, scientists using powerful telescopes had learned quite a bit about the Moon. They knew the Moon is made of rock and has no *atmosphere*. They had studied the mountains, plains, and *craters* on the Moon's surface. They had even calculated the Moon's *density* and determined that the force of *gravity* is weaker on the Moon than on Earth. From what they saw, scientists also deduced its population—zero.

What about the areas they couldn't see, though? Could there be life on the side of the Moon that always faces away from Earth?

Earth's Moon, our closest neighbor

In addition, scientists still had many questions about what the Moon's polar regions were like. They also wondered about the texture of the Moon's surface and were curious about how the Moon had formed.

In 1959, the first robotic spacecraft traveled from Earth to the Moon. The images they sent back to Earth allowed us to see and study the Moon's poles and hidden regions close up. Then, in 1969, the first people traveled to the Moon. Most of the information gathered by the astronauts confirmed the theories developed by scientists who had studied the Moon from Earth.

More recently, spacecraft have helped scientists collect information about many of the moons that *orbit* other planets in our solar system. Each of these moons has a tale to tell. Studying distant worlds has helped us gain a better understanding of and appreciation for our own planet. Scientists now know more about how Earth formed, how it changed throughout history, and the importance of maintaining its ecosystems.

## Where Did Moons Come From?

About 4.6 billion years ago, in the galaxy known to us as the Milky Way, a star was born out of a swirling cloud of hot gas and dust. That star was our Sun. This infant star was surrounded by a huge, hot *mass* of spinning gases and debris. As these materials gradually cooled, they condensed into larger and smaller masses. Some of the masses stuck together and eventually became planets. Over time, the planets grew larger and attracted smaller masses to them. These smaller worlds danced like partners around the planets. The smaller worlds closest to the giant planets remained seething hot and molten. Those farther away became frozen and still. All these are the bodies we now call moons.

Not all of the debris came under the influence of the planets, however. Trillions of chunks of rock and ice developed into the *asteroids, comets,* and *meteoroids* that also orbit the Sun.

# The Planets

## Vital Statistics

| Planet | Diameter* | Distance from the Sun (AU)† | Number of Known Moons |
|---|---|---|---|
| MERCURY | 3,032 miles (4,880 km) | 0.39 | 0 |
| VENUS | 7,519 miles (12,100 km) | 0.72 | 0 |
| EARTH | 7,926 miles (12,756 km) | 1.00 | 1 |
| MARS | 4,217 miles (6,787 km) | 1.52 | 2 |
| JUPITER | 88,846 miles (142,984 km) | 5.2 | 16 |
| SATURN | 74,975 miles (120,660 km) | 9.5 | 18 |
| URANUS | 31,765 miles (51,120 km) | 19.16 | 17 |
| NEPTUNE | 30,777 miles (49,530 km) | 30.0 | 8 |
| PLUTO | 1,429 miles (2,300 km) | 30.4 | 1 |

*The *diameter* of a circular object is the width, or distance, across its center.

†AU is an abbreviation for the term *astronomical unit,* a measurement used to express distance between objects in space. 1 AU equals the distance between Earth and the Sun.

"Shooting stars" like the streak in this photo are really meteors—
flashes of light from meteoroids entering our planet's atmosphere.

An asteroid is a piece of rocky debris. Scientists have discovered more than 7,000 asteroids, and hundreds more are spotted each year. There are probably millions of others that are too small to see with telescopes. A wide band of asteroids called the *asteroid belt* is located between Mars and Jupiter, but not all asteroids are in the asteroid belt.

A group of asteroids called the Trojans is located close to Jupiter. A few asteroids, known as the Centaurs, have been discovered close to the planet Neptune. The Amor asteroids intersect Mars's orbit, while the Apollo asteroids and Atens asteroids cross Earth's orbit. Recently, scientists have discovered that at least one asteroid has a moon of its own.

Comets are small balls of rock and ice that travel toward the Sun in long orbits that originate on the remote outer edge of the solar system. When a comet gets close to the Sun, some of its ice melts and releases gases. These gases form a tail behind the comet.

When a comet or asteroid is hit by another object in space, it may break into many small pieces. These pieces are called meteoroids.

Once part of a meteoroid in space, this chunk of stony iron is a meteorite.

When a meteoroid enters the atmosphere of a planet or moon, it creates a flash of light known as a *meteor*. Some people call meteors "shooting stars," but a meteor is not a star. When a meteoroid lands on a planet or moon, it is called a *meteorite*.

Meteorite collisions have decreased since the early days of the solar system, but they have not stopped. The solar system is still a place where objects smack into each other like billiard balls.

Sketches of the Moon drawn by Galileo

## How Do We Find Out about Moons?

Nearly 400 years ago, an Italian scientist named Galileo Galilei first pointed a telescope at the nighttime sky. He thought taking a closer look at the stars and planets might unravel some of the mysteries of our Universe, and he was right. Galileo discovered four moons orbiting Jupiter. He also made the first detailed observations of our own Moon. Telescopes soon became every astronomer's greatest resource.

In the late 1950s, the space age dawned. In the 1960s, we sent spacecraft to the Moon. By the early 1970s, we began sending spacecraft with names like *Pioneer, Voyager,* and *Pathfinder* to gather data about the other planets in our solar system. These spacecraft provided close-up images and new information that completely changed our ideas about the moons and planets orbiting our Sun.

In 1990, astronauts aboard the Space Shuttle launched a powerful telescope that would have amazed Galileo. As the school-bus-sized Hubble Space Telescope orbits Earth, it gathers extraordinary new information about the Universe, including the moons of our solar system.

## The Voyage Begins

This book will take you on an incredible voyage to the moons that orbit the planets in our solar system. It will be a fascinating journey unequaled in any travel agency's brochures. You will witness incredible heat, violent volcanoes, and merciless cold and experience the loneliness of distant worlds. You will encounter airless, dusty spheres and age-old scars caused by meteorite impacts. Above all, you will find tremendous diversity and make many fascinating discoveries.

# Chapter 2

# Moons of the Inner Planets

## Missions to the Moon

In October 1957, the former Union of Soviet Socialist Republics (USSR) launched *Sputnik*, the first artificial *satellite* to orbit Earth. Only 2 years later, the USSR sent the first spacecraft to Earth's Moon, which some people call Luna. *Luna 1* carried no passengers, but its instruments collected all kinds of information about the world closest to Earth. As time passed, the USSR and the United States sent dozens of spacecraft to the Moon. Some orbited the Moon, while others landed on the surface. They took photos that showed us what the terrain was like and collected data that allowed scientists to determine what the surface was made of.

*Apollo 11* astronauts Neil Armstrong (left), Michael Collins (center), and Buzz Aldrin (right). Armstrong and Aldrin were the first humans to set foot on the Moon.

On July 20, 1969, Neil Armstrong spoke those now-famous words, "That's one small step for [a] man, one giant leap for mankind." It was a giant leap. Before he and Edwin "Buzz" Aldrin arrived on the Moon, no human being had ever set foot on another world anywhere in the Universe. Along with crewmate Michael Collins who was patiently orbiting above them, Armstrong and Aldrin made history. More than 1 billion people in countries throughout the world watched the landing on television.

*Apollo 15* astronaut Alfred M. Worden snapped this photo of Aristarchus Crater (top right), Herodotus Crater (bottom right), and Schroter's Valley (bottom center).

A total of six Apollo spacecraft carried astronauts to the Moon. They returned to Earth with sample rocks and stories of what they saw as they trekked about or traveled across the surface in lunar rovers.

## Craters, Mountains, Valleys, and Lava

When scientists studied the photographs the astronauts took of the Moon's surface, they realized that the Moon's mountains are not nearly as rugged and jagged as they look from Earth. Because the Sun's light hits the surface of the Moon at a low angle, it creates long and angular shadows. These shadows gave scientists the wrong impression of the Moon's terrain. In reality, the features of the Moon's surface are fairly rounded because they have been hammered down by endless meteorite strikes.

The hundreds of thousands of deep craters on the Moon's surface indicate that it underwent intense bombardment in the distant past—probably between 4.4 and 4 billion years ago. Some craters are huge. A crater called Tycho is as large as Yellowstone National Park in Wyoming. Long valleys or trenches are also common on the surface of the Moon. One of the best-known valleys is Hadley *Rille*.

Areas that look dark from Earth are broad, level plains that were smoothed by ancient lava flows. Some ancient astronomers thought these areas might be seas filled with water, so scientists gave them such names as the Sea of Serenity and the Sea of Showers. Neil Armstrong and Buzz Aldrin landed on an area of the moon called the Sea of Tranquillity.

Huge boulders and rocky rubble are scattered over the Moon's surface. A layer of deep, powdery dust and rock chips covers nearly everything. With every step they took, the astronauts left behind clear footprints on this layer, called *regolith*.

The footprints the astronauts made on the Moon's unchanging surface will last for millions of years.

It's hard to imagine just how desolate and still the Moon really is. The astronauts said they were startled by the incredible silence. There were no birds singing, no leaves rustling, and, of course, no noise from traffic. In fact, there was no sound at all. On Earth, sound waves travel through the atmosphere, but the Moon has almost no atmosphere. It has very little atmosphere because it has very little gravity. Gravity is an invisible force that pulls objects toward the center of a world. Earth's gravity keeps our planet's atmosphere in place. Since gravity is very weak on the Moon, nearly all the gases that may once have surrounded it have long since disappeared.

The Moon's surface has changed very little over time. There is no running water to carve gurgling brooks down the Moon's slopes or fill its broad, shallow basins. Because the Moon has so little atmosphere, there is no weather—no rain or wind—to cause erosion. The Moon does not have any geologic activity either. There are no erupting volcanoes or spewing geysers. For these reasons, the footprints made by astronauts in 1969 will remain unchanged on the Moon's surface for thousands, perhaps even millions, of years.

## The First and Only Lunar Field Geologist

So far, Harrison H. Schmitt (1935– ) is the only scientist ever to visit the surface of a moon. During the late 1960s, Jack (as his friends call him) taught Apollo astronauts what to look for when they searched for rock samples on the surface of Earth's Moon. Finally, his turn came when *Apollo 17*—the last Apollo flight—headed to the Moon on December 7, 1972.

At the time, Jack Schmitt was 37 years old and had just finished jet airplane and helicopter pilot training programs. He had studied at the California Institute of Technology in Pasadena, California, and had earned a doctorate in geology from Harvard University in Boston, Massachusetts. He had also received a Fulbright fellowship that allowed him to continue his studies in Oslo, Norway. When Jack went to the Moon, he put all his education and training to good use.

Schmitt and fellow astronaut Eugene Cernan landed in a narrow box canyon, surrounded by the ridges of the Taurus Mountains. As he stepped out for his first close-up of the Moon's Taurus-Littrow Valley, Schmitt exclaimed, "It's a good geologist's paradise if I've ever seen one!"

The region was rich in geological finds. Schmitt and Cernan spent 75 hours on the surface of the Moon. For 22 of those hours, the men hiked or drove across the Moon's rugged terrain.

Schmitt later became United States Senator from New Mexico, serving from 1977 through 1982. Since that time, he has had a varied career as writer, lecturer, consultant, and teacher in fields related to space, geology, risk, and policy.

Astronaut Jack Schmitt (top left) poses with other members of the *Apollo 17* crew.

## Inside Luna

From instruments placed on the Moon by Apollo astronauts, scientists learned that the Moon is mostly solid. Like Earth, the Moon has a *crust,* a *mantle,* and a *core.* The crust, or outer surface, is hard and rocky. On the side of the Moon that faces Earth, the crust is 40 miles (64 kilometers) thick. The crust on the far side of the Moon is even thicker.

The Moon's mantle—the region just below the crust—is composed of solid rock and is about 600 miles (1,000 km) thick. The Moon's central core is about 870 miles (1,400 km) thick. Some *planetologists*— scientists who study planets, moons, and other objects in space—think the core is completely solid, but others think it may have a consistency similar to cooked oatmeal.

## Where Did Earth's Moon Come From?

Everybody knows that Earth is the "third rock from the Sun." Counting out from the Sun, though, Earth is also the first planet with a satellite. Neither Mercury nor Venus has a moon. Of the four inner planets, only Earth has a large, spherical Moon. The two moons that orbit Mars are small and oddly shaped.

Earth's Moon is unlike most other moons because it is fairly close to Earth—only about 238,860 miles (384,400 km)—and relatively large. The Moon is the fifth largest moon in the solar system, and about one-fourth as big as Earth. In fact, the Moon is so large relative to Earth that many scientists think of Earth and the Moon as a double-planet system.

What could have caused this strange relationship? Maybe our Moon did not form in the same way as other moons in our solar system. Scientists have struggled with this question for many years and have come up with several possible theories.

According to the fission theory or "spun-off chunk" theory, Earth's rapid *rotation,* or spinning on its *axis,* caused a huge chunk of Earth to break off early in the planet's formation. The broken chunk snapped away from the infant Earth with enough force to send it flying into orbit, and it became the Moon. This cataclysmic event would have left a gaping hole in the surface of Earth—and just such a hole does exist where the Pacific Ocean now lies. However, the composition of the ocean floor does not match the Moon's *composition.*

The capture, or "gotcha," theory presents another story plot. Maybe a huge asteroid or a small, wandering planet came too close to Earth and was captured by Earth's gravity. The smaller body had enough momentum to avoid tumbling to Earth's surface, but not enough to break free of Earth's gravity. As a result, it became locked in orbit, where we see it today as Earth's Moon.

In the co-formation, or "sister," theory, two chunks of material formed at the same time out of the ancient cloud of dust and gases. They remained separate because the larger one was not quite massive enough to force the smaller one to combine with it. However, the smaller one—the Moon—did come under the gravitational influence of the larger one, Earth.

More recently, a new theory has gained popularity. This theory uses newly gathered information of the Moon and computer modeling to predict what might have happened during the solar system's early formation. Computer models show that during Earth's early history, a runaway planet—perhaps as large as Mars—may have crashed into Earth while our planet was still hot and molten. The collision sent large amounts of steaming, liquid material into space. The material could not escape Earth's gravitational pull and began spinning around

The word "theory" has a way of coming up in everyday conversation and popping up in newspaper headlines. You probably have a vague idea of what it means, but do you know what it means when scientists use it?

For scientists, a theory generally begins as a *hypothesis*. A hypothesis is a statement, or premise, that a researcher believes is worth exploring. It has to be more than just an interesting idea, though. A hypothesis must be stated in such a way that the researcher can prove it true or false by conducting experiments or making observations.

A hypothesis has to hold up over time and be testable by many scientists. If the results are consistently valid, a hypothesis becomes a scientific theory.

Even then, the testing is not over. A good theory makes "predictions" —events that researchers can look for as a further test of its validity. By the time textbooks carry discussions of a well-known theory, such as Einstein's theory of relativity or Copernicus's theory that the planets revolve around the Sun, it has survived extensive testing and verification. No scientific theory can ever be accepted as completely "proven," however. It must always remain open to further tests and scrutiny as new facts or observations emerge.

the planet. At first, it may have formed a disk of floating debris, but eventually it condensed into a single Moon.

According to the computer model, such an impact would mean that most of the material shot into space came from Earth's surface. If this theory is valid, the Moon's composition should resemble Earth's surface. Overall, the Moon does resemble Earth's crust much more than its inner layers. For example, Earth's core is rich in iron, but the Moon has very little iron, even at its core. If the Moon had formed at the same time as Earth did, and from roughly the same materials, its inner layers would be more like Earth's inner layers. Many scientists also support this new theory because Earth's Moon is quite different from the moons of Mars. If the Moon was formed by a chance, one-of-a-kind occurrence, it is not surprising that it is such an oddball.

## Ice on the Moon!

In the 1990s, two more spacecraft gave scientists a chance to study the Moon very closely. *Clementine* surveyed the surface of the Moon from 1994 to 1996, and *Lunar Prospector* began sending back new information in early 1998. The Moon made the headlines once again, and this time the big news was ice! These spacecraft revealed that ice almost certainly exists on the Moon. Recent estimates show that as much as 544 billion tons of frozen water may lie hidden in its deep, shadowed crevices.

Scientists believe the Moon's ice came from comets. At some point in the Moon's past, one or more comets must have struck our Moon. The heat of the impact would have melted the comet's ice

Scientists compare comets like this one to huge, dirty snowballs—and they think they may be the source of frozen water found on the Moon.

and sent vapor flying in every direction. In areas of the Moon that are exposed to the Sun, the vapor would have evaporated and disappeared. However, some regions of the moon never face the Sun. The permanent subfreezing temperatures in these regions would have trapped the water as a fine frost. Images taken by *Clementine* and *Lunar Prospector* showed scientists that frost.

Many people were very excited by this discovery. It meant researchers or settlers could live on the Moon without having to transport vast quantities of water from Earth.

## The Moons of Mars: Hostages from the Asteroid Belt?

Leaving Earth's Moon, you see Mars in the distance. Mars is the fourth planet from the Sun and the last of the *terrestrial* planets. In 1877, American astronomer Asaph Hall discovered that Mars has two very small moons—Phobos and Deimos. Phobos measures only 17 miles (27 km) across, and Deimos is just 9.3 miles (15 km) in diameter.

Four spacecraft photographed Phobos in the 1970s and 1980s. *Mariner 9*, *Viking 1*, and *Viking 2* were all launched by the United States. *Phobos 2* was launched by the USSR in 1988. *Viking 2* also flew very close to Deimos and sent back images. However, the most exciting views of both moons came in 1998 from the *Mars Global Surveyor*.

These images showed hip-deep dust on the surface of Phobos. Scientists believe the dust is the result of meteoroids crashing on this little moon over millions of years. Steep crater slopes on Phobos show evidence of landslides. This finding surprised scientists because Phobos's gravity is a thousand times weaker than Earth's gravity.

Like Earth's Moon, both Phobos and Deimos are locked into position, so Mars's moons always keep the same face toward the red planet. These small, dark moons seem to be made of the same carbon-rich rock as many meteorites. They are roughly triangular in shape, with the long side pointing toward the planet.

The size, shape, and composition of Phobos and Deimos make some scientists suspect that they started out as asteroids. They may have been knocked off-course by a gravitational tug from the giant planet Jupiter and captured by Mars in the early days of the smaller planet's formation. Other scientists think they may have broken off from larger objects during a collision. No one is really sure where or how the moons originated.

# Moons of the Inner Planets

## Vital Statistics

| Moon (Planet) | Diameter | Distance from Center of Planet | Surface Composition | Discovery |
|---|---|---|---|---|
| MOON/LUNA (EARTH) | 2,160 miles (3,476 km) | 238,860 miles (384,330 km) from Earth | Volcanic dust and rock | Prehistoric |
| PHOBOS (MARS) | 17 miles (27 km) | 5,830 miles (9,380 km) from Mars | Carbon-rich rock and ice | 1877 |
| DEIMOS (MARS) | 9.3 miles (15 km) | 14,580 miles (23,460 km) from Mars | Carbon-rich rock and ice | 1877 |

Of the two moons, Phobos is bigger. Its crater-covered surface suggests that it has been heavily bombarded by asteroids and meteoroids. At least one of those impacts nearly destroyed the moon. One giant crater, known as Stickney, is so deep and so massive that it makes the satellite look like a vase! Deep, grooved fractures extending from the crater indicate the violence of the impact that created Stickney. Near the crater, these fractures are 2,300 feet (700 meters) wide and 295 feet (90 m) deep.

Phobos hovers uncomfortably close to Mars— only about 3,700 miles (6,000 km) from the Martian surface. No other moon in the solar system orbits so close to its planet. The little moon zips around Mars in just 7 hours and 39 minutes. So, in one Martian day, you might see Phobos

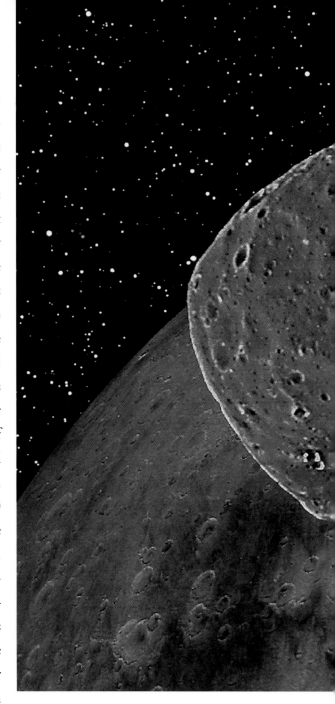

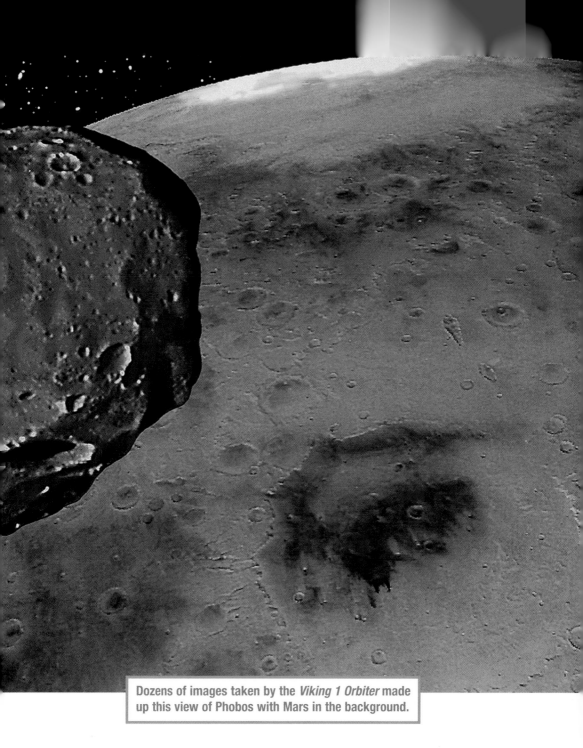

Dozens of images taken by the *Viking 1 Orbiter* made up this view of Phobos with Mars in the background.

rise, speed across the sky, and set—twice. Phobos is slowly moving even closer to Mars. Scientists predict that Phobos will crash into the red planet sometime in the next 50 million years.

Deimos is farther from Mars. The surface of this smaller moon appears almost entirely smooth because its craters are filled with a powdery debris. Why is the surface of Deimos smooth, when Phobos is so craggy? Scientists think that when objects crashed into Deimos, the debris was not hurled out into space. It was attracted by Deimos's gravity, and eventually fell back to the moon's surface. The debris that ricocheted off Phobos probably ended up on the surface of Mars because Phobos is so close to Mars and because Mars's gravity is so much stronger.

In the future, these two little moons could play important roles as way stations for expeditions to Mars or space stations designed to study the Martian surface.

## Leaving the Inner Planets

As you leave the rocky planets behind and head toward the gas giants of the outer solar system, you will cross through the asteroid belt. On your way, you may encounter Dactyl, a small moon that orbits around an

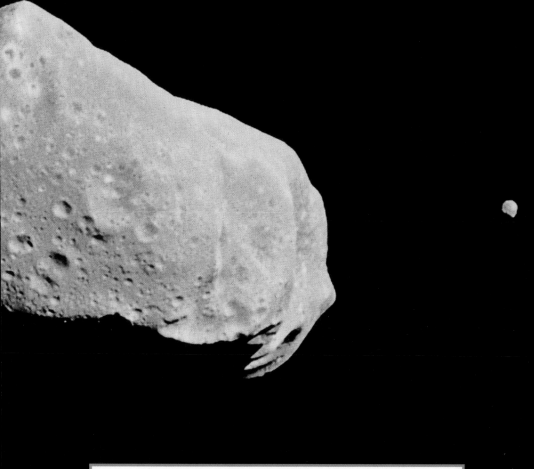

The spacecraft *Galileo* captured this image of the asteroid Ida and its tiny moon Dactyl—the first asteroid–moon duo ever discovered.

asteroid called Ida, or you may see the moon that travels around the asteroid Eugenia.

Your next stop will be the Jupiter system. There you will encounter many strange moons. Some are hot and violent, while others are cold and icy. One may even have an ocean teeming with primitive life.

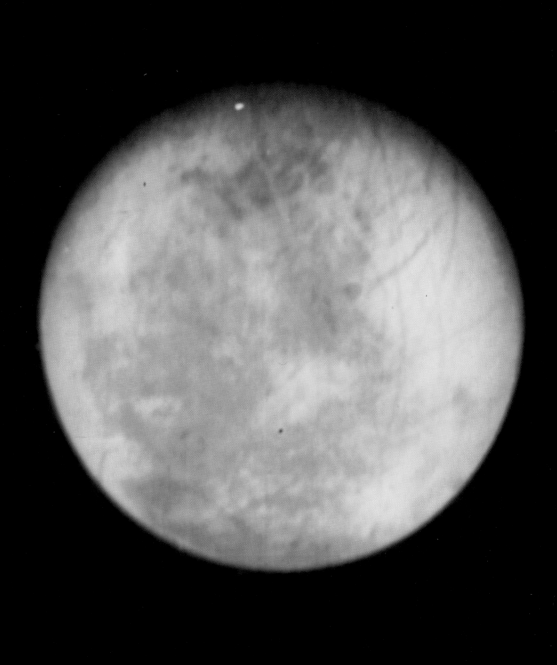

**Does this distant world have an ocean thriving with life?**

# 3

# Jupiter's Moons: Worlds of Heat and Ice

I magine a boiling-hot world far from Earth, peppered with volcanoes and rivers of molten rock. Scalding gases and liquid spurt far into space. Steaming fluids spill out of volcanoes and ooze across land areas as vast as Arizona. From a distance, this world looks a lot like a giant, bubbling pizza.

Picture another globe spinning nearby. Its icy white surface seems unblemished and smooth, except for a few strange crisscrossing grooves. Some scientists think that a warm ocean of water may lie below this outer coat of ice. Believe it or not, that ocean might even harbor forms of life!

Think of yet another strange world—this one with a complex, mixed-up exterior. The hodgepodge surface is dark and heavily cratered in some areas. These regions have been repeatedly pounded by falling meteoroids, leaving deep holes that appear to have been made by giant sledgehammers. Other areas of the surface are smoother and lighter in color, with many grooves and ridges.

A fourth sphere circles silently nearby. It is nearly as black as coal and pocked by giant craters. One vast crater measures as far across as the distance from San Francisco to Los Angeles and is surrounded by huge circles, like a giant bull's-eye in the sky.

You may think these descriptions are scenes from a science-fiction movie, but they aren't. These fantastic worlds are real. They are four of the moons that orbit Jupiter, the king of the planets.

# The Galilean Moons
## Vital Statistics

| Moon | Diameter | Distance from Center of Jupiter | Surface Composition | Discovery |
|------|----------|-------------------------------|--------------------|-----------|
| Io | 2,259 miles (3,636 km) | 261,970 miles (421,600 km) | Sulfur | 1610 |
| Europa | 1,939 miles (3,120 km) | 416,900 miles (670,900 km) | Frozen water | 1610 |
| Ganymede | 3,273 miles (5,268 km) | 664,900 miles (1,070,000 km) | Dirty ice | 1610 |
| Callisto | 2,994 miles (4,818 km) | 1,170,000 miles (1,883,000 km) | Dirty ice | 1610 |

NASA put together this Jupiter family portrait from separate Voyager images of the giant planet and its four largest moons—Io, Europa, Ganymede, and Callisto.

## In the Grip of a Giant

Io, Europa, Ganymede, and Callisto are Jupiter's four largest moons. Along with Jupiter's other twelve known moons, they form a remarkable family. Like members of a human family, these sixteen moons are all different, but they influence one another. Both individually and as a group, Jupiter's moons are the main characters in many fascinating stories.

Jupiter's orbit is about five times farther from the Sun than Earth's orbit. Jupiter is the fifth planet from the Sun and the closest of the *gas giants*—the huge planets composed entirely, or almost entirely, of gas. Saturn, Uranus, and Neptune are also gas giants.

Jupiter is enormous. It is nearly 88,846 miles (142,984 km) across, making it the largest planet in our solar system. If Jupiter were a gigantic hollow ball, more than 1,000 Earth-sized planets could fit inside it. In fact, if you could crush all the planets into a fine powder and pour the powder into that hollow ball, there would still be plenty of room left over.

Of course, Jupiter isn't a gigantic hollow ball. It is a rapidly rotating mass with a huge atmosphere. The enormous mass of this planet exerts an intense gravitational pull on nearby objects. Jupiter's tremendous gravity is largely responsible for the varied history of its colorful moons.

## The Galilean Moons: Discovery and Early Exploration

Astronomers have known about the four largest moons of Jupiter for nearly 400 years. As you learned in Chapter 1, the first person to spot them was Galileo. As he scanned the night sky with his newly built telescope, he turned the instrument's lens toward a speck of light that every astronomer knew was the planet called Jupiter. Galileo found a surprise.

Near the giant planet's edge, he spotted three much smaller dots of light. A few nights later, he spied a fourth tiny dot. At first, Galileo thought the dots were stars. However, he noticed that as Jupiter moved across the sky, so did the dots. Galileo also observed that the dots seemed

## How Science Works: The Power of Observation

Galileo Galilei was the first person to use a telescope to look at the star-filled sky. Besides studying Earth's Moon and finding Jupiter's four largest moons, he also discovered sunspots—dark spots on the Sun.

Galileo's discoveries led him to question the widely accepted theory explaining the arrangement of objects in the Universe. In the 1600s, most Europeans believed Earth was the center of the Universe. They thought the Sun, the planets, and all other objects in space revolved around our planet. But Galileo began to believe an idea proposed in the mid-1500s by a Polish scientist named Nicolaus Copernicus.

Copernicus had claimed that the Sun—not Earth—is at the center of our solar system. Because this hypothesis challenged the view accepted by scientists and religious officials, and because Copernicus had no physical proof, most people paid little attention to his work.

Galileo's discovery of Jupiter's moons provided proof of Copernicus's theory—proof based on direct observation. People could look through a telescope and see for themselves that these moons were moving around another planet, not around

Earth. Galileo was a respected university professor and an eloquent speaker, and he presented his ideas all over Europe.

In 1616, however, authorities of the Roman Catholic Church ordered Galileo to stop spreading ideas that disagreed with their teachings. This was not an easy order for Galileo to obey. He was a scientist and an outspoken man. Keeping quiet was hard for him. In 1632, he published his ideas in a book called *Dialogue on the Two Chief World Systems*.

Church authorities were furious. Galileo was put on trial and, eventually, forced to retract his views. He spent the rest of his life under house arrest, and almost every copy of his book was burned. Galileo died in 1642.

Because the Roman Catholic Church opposed Galileo publicly, very few people accepted Galileo's view of the solar system. They simply refused to believe that the planets *revolve* around the Sun. As time passed, however, many scientists began to realize that Galileo—and Copernicus—had been right. In 1992, 350 years after the scientist's death, Pope John Paul II admitted on behalf of the Catholic Church that Galileo had been wronged.

to move around the planet. He realized that he was looking at moons revolving around another world. Today Io, Europa, Ganymede, and Callisto are known as the "Galilean moons," in honor of their discoverer.

## Io: The Big Squeeze

Io is about the same size as Earth's Moon, but the two moons look very different. Images of Io show a mottled yellow and orange ball that looks a lot like a big pizza with cheese, tomato sauce, and a few black olives. Photographs taken by *Voyager 1* showed that Io has hundreds of volcanoes.

The most startling images show a burst of color spurting from Io's surface against the black background of space. These photos prove that some of the volcanoes on Io are still active! Many scientists consider this the most important discovery of the Voyager missions.

Io's volcanoes are violent and dramatic. Molten material spews into space at speeds up to 2,300 miles (3,700 km) per hour. Compare this to Mount Etna, a volcano on Earth. Mount Etna, which is located on the island of Sicily, coughs up steam, smoke, and ash at only 112 miles (180 km) per hour. Because the force of gravity is six times weaker on Io than on Earth, volcanic plumes often spout materials more than 160 miles (260 km) into space. That's farther than the distance between Boston, Massachusetts, and Albany, New York.

In 1995, images from the Hubble Space Telescope showed scientists that an enormous new volcano had formed on Io since the Voyager space probes flew by. The *Galileo* spacecraft, named after the moons' discoverer, was launched in 1989 from the Space Shuttle *Atlantis*. After arriving at Jupiter in 1996, it explored the Jupiter system up close. The probe sent back all kinds of images and data about all four Galilean moons.

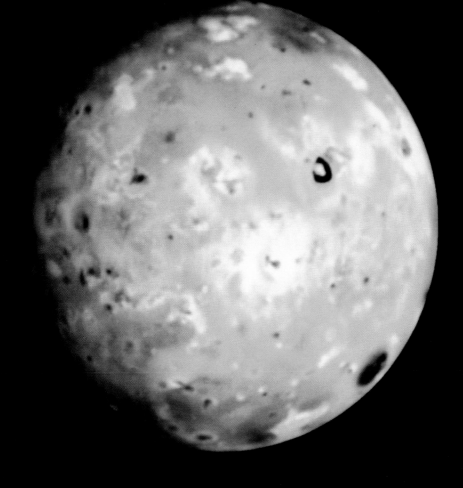

This 1996 *Galileo* image of Io shows few traces of impact craters. That's because active volcanoes spew molten lava that constantly smooths the moon's ruddy surface.

*Galileo* provided a close-up view of dozens of sulfur-spewing volcanoes on Jupiter's fiery moon Io. The probe showed huge new lakes of molten sulfur lapping against steaming shores. New volcanic cones studded the moon's surface. In fact, Io has so many active volcanoes that their flowing lava has completely erased all signs of meteoroid impacts.

The probe also discovered that the lava spewing from the moon's volcanoes is sizzling hot—hotter than any eruption on Earth has been for billions of years. The lava erupting from a volcano called Pillan Patera was 3,140 degrees Fahrenheit (1,730 degrees Celsius). Except for the Sun, no other body in the solar system has such high temperatures.

Recent photos show a rash of glowing red lava pools on Io's surface. Above some of the erupting volcanoes, a bluish glow appears, and high above, huge power surges of more than 400,000 volts generate bright arcs of light. What causes all this violent activity? The best guess is a combination of forces caused by Jupiter and nearby moons.

Of the four Galilean moons, Io is the closest to Jupiter. Because Jupiter is much larger than Earth, its gravity is much stronger. Jupiter's gravitational pull is two and a half times greater than Earth's. In fact, no planet in the solar system has a stronger gravitational pull than Jupiter. The area of space affected by a planet's gravitational force is

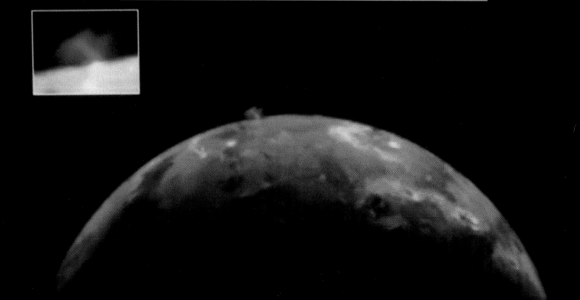

*Galileo* caught this color-enhanced view of Jupiter's moon Io just as one of its volcanoes spewed blue material into space. For an even more detailed view, see the inset in the upper left of the photo.

called its *gravitational field*. Jupiter's mighty gravitational field exerts a huge drag on Io.

The moons Europa and Ganymede also tug at Io. Locked in a dance with these moons, Io makes two trips around Jupiter for every orbit completed by Europa. In turn, Europa makes two orbits for every orbit completed by Ganymede.

Because Jupiter, Europa, and Ganymede all pull on Io, its surface bulges as much as 328 feet (100 m) as the hot molten materials deep inside the moon shift back and forth. Io is one of the few places in the solar system that has tides, but no water.

Io is, indeed, a strange and violent world. As far as scientists know, it is like no other place in the solar system. It has so many fascinating features because it is so close to Jupiter. The tremendous gravitational pull of the king of the planets is responsible for the small moon's colorful geology.

## Europa: Oceans and Life?

At first glance, Io's closest neighbor, Europa, seems bland by comparison. As you will soon learn, however, this smooth-faced moon has a mystery and intrigue of its own.

In images taken by *Voyager 2*, Europa looked like a smooth, white billiard ball marked with vague, pale lines. Just slightly smaller than our own Moon, Europa's surface is often as cold as –260°F (–162°C). This moon, which is about ten times brighter than Earth's Moon, initially seemed to be a bleak, frozen, featureless world.

Today, scientists have a different view of Europa. In fact, some even call this moon the "gem of the solar system." After poring over images of Europa, scientists began to notice what was missing—what

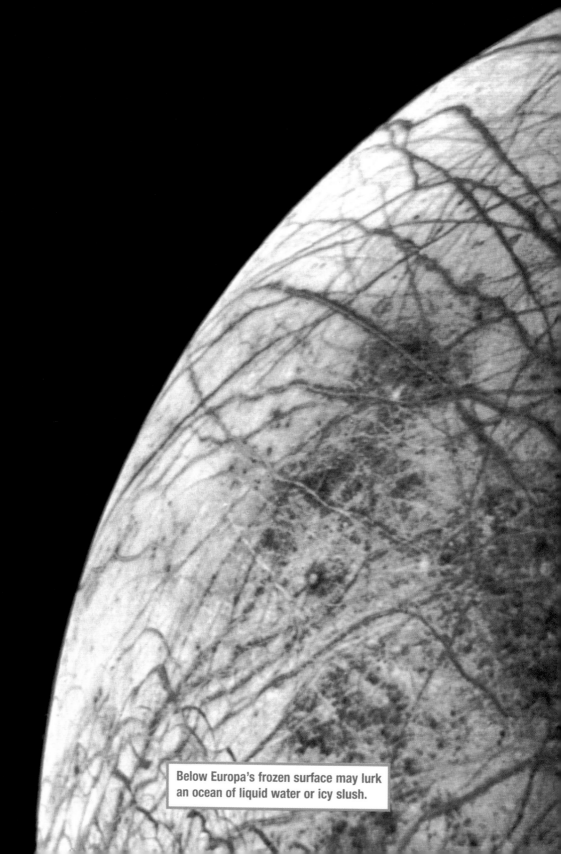

Below Europa's frozen surface may lurk
an ocean of liquid water or icy slush.

they didn't see. Europa has no craters. How could this be? Every object in the solar system has been pummeled by meteoroids and other passing objects for billions of years. The absence of craters could only mean that some process had erased the signs of these impacts.

Images taken by the *Galileo* spacecraft in 1997 transformed our view of Europa. Some scientists began to speculate that an ocean of water or ice-and-water slush lies beneath the moon's icy crust.

What makes scientists think there is an ocean on this moon? By analyzing the light emitted from Europa, scientists learned that its surface is made up of frozen water. Researchers believe that this blanket of frozen water is more than 60 miles (97 km) thick in some places. As early as 1979, *Voyager 2* images hinted that far below the surface the moon's interior might be warm enough to melt ice.

Photos taken by *Galileo* in 1997 provided additional clues. Some of the images showed a crater that is 16 miles (26 km) across, but very shallow. In fact, the floor of Pwyll crater is nearly level with Europa's surface. Yet the meteoroid that formed the crater hit hard enough to plow into the moon's interior and throw out dark material. If Europa were made of solid ice, this impact should have made a dent at least as deep as the Grand Canyon. Because the crater is now so shallow, scientists suspect that fluid material from below the surface seeped up and filled in the crater almost immediately.

Images taken by both *Voyager 2* and *Galileo* revealed that large areas of Europa's surface are covered with chunky, textured, iceberglike structures as large as a city block. In addition, photos from *Galileo* showed features between the huge ice rafts that could have been covered with slush or a liquid material at one time. Could Europa's icy surface have broken apart and then refrozen?

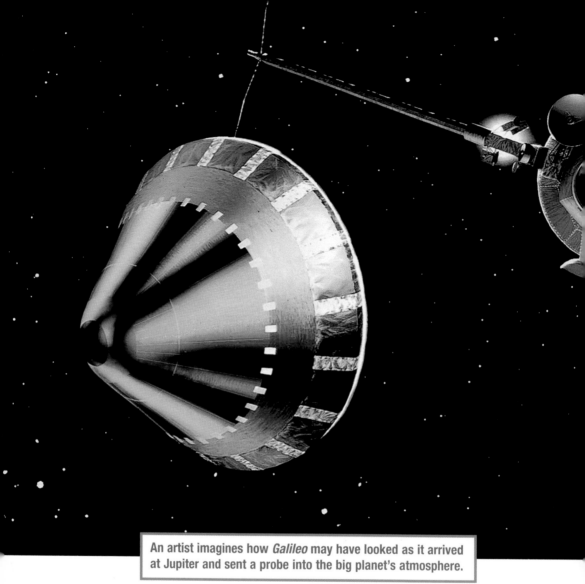

An artist imagines how *Galileo* may have looked as it arrived at Jupiter and sent a probe into the big planet's atmosphere.

Between continent-sized plates of ice, *Galileo* detected dark, wedge-shaped areas that could represent new icy crust. The ridges and parallel grooves that scar these surfaces look similar to newly formed crust on the Earth's seafloor. On our planet, new seafloor forms in places where molten lava from deep within Earth creeps up to the ocean floor. On Europa, new crust may form when water or slush creeps up to the moon's surface.

How could such a cold world have an ocean of liquid water? No one knows the answer to this question. Some scientists claim that the gravitational fields of Jupiter and some of its moons cause Europa's surface to flex and bend and its interior to move and swell as it orbits Jupiter, the king of the planets. This movement could cause heat to build up deep inside Europa. Maybe all that heat melts enough ice to form a liquid ocean beneath the moon's icy surface. According to some estimates, this ocean could be ten times deeper than the Pacific Ocean, the deepest ocean on Earth.

If Europa's ocean contains liquid water that has been warmed by heat generated in the moon's interior as well as organic materials deposited by meteoroid impacts, it has everything necessary for life to develop. Could very simple life forms exist on Europa? If they do, Europa would really be "the gem of the solar system." Discovering life on one of Jupiter's moon could be the most dramatic and profound discovery in the history of humankind!

## Ganymede: The Cratered Giant

Ganymede is an icy giant. It is larger than the planets Mercury and Pluto, and about one-third the size of Earth. With a diameter of 3,273 miles (5,268 km), Ganymede is the largest known moon in the solar system.

Images taken by *Voyager 2* gave scientists their first close glimpses of this alien world. The spacecraft's photos revealed a puzzling place full of icy craters and deeply grooved surfaces. More recently, *Galileo* provided even better images.

Jupiter's largest moon, Ganymede, is marked by dark, cratered areas and brighter, smoother regions.

A chain of thirteen craters on the surface suggest that the moon was struck by a fragmented object at some point in its long history. Perhaps a passing comet came too close to Jupiter and was pulled to pieces by the big planet's gravitational force. Then as the fractured comet whipped past the king of the planets, it plowed into Ganymede. The craters left by that impact look like a string of pearls on the big moon's surface.

If this scenario is accurate, it would not be the only time that a comet was broken apart by Jupiter. In 1994, fragments of the comet Shoemaker-Levy 9 collided with the king of the planets.

Images of Ganymede indicate that the moon is geologically complex. Ganymede has two different kinds of terrain. About 40 percent of its surface is covered by dark, heavily cratered regions, ancient volcanic deposits, and other geological remnants of a much more active past. These areas are believed to be part of Ganymede's original surface.

The rest of the moon, which scientists think is newer, is smoother, lighter in color, and has many grooves and ridges. Some of the grooves are thousands of miles long, and some of the ridges are 2,300 feet (700 m) high. At times, the ridges and grooves look as though they've been twisted. The craters in these are unusually shallow, unlike the deep valleys of many craters on Earth's Moon. Some scientists believe that the mountains and valleys on Ganymede's frozen surface may sometimes evaporate or crumble away, smoothing the ruggedness of its features.

Images taken by *Galileo* have led scientists to believe that, about 3 billion years ago, Ganymede may have had an ocean below its icy crust. The crust appears to have fractured, causing water volcanoes and rivers to gush out and then quickly freeze in place, re-forming the surface. Today the big moon is frozen solid. Scientists don't know whether life ever existed on Ganymede, but they do know that all the necessary ingredients—heat, liquid water, and organic material—were probably present at one time.

## Callisto: Pock-Marked Ball of Blackened Ice

Callisto is the outermost of the Galilean moons. Its orbit is 1,170,000 miles (1,883,000 km) from the center of Jupiter. Scientists believe that Callisto has changed very little over the last 4 billion years. Of all the objects we have observed in our solar system, Callisto has the oldest and most heavily cratered surface. Callisto is so crowded with impact craters that no object could strike the planet without hitting a crater that already exists.

Some craters are surrounded by large concentric circles, making it seem as if the incoming meteoroid sent out giant ripples of material at the moment of impact. These ripples have remained immobile for billions of years. The slow movement of ice on Callisto's surface has blurred them only slightly.

Callisto is a big moon—the third largest in the solar system. The planet Mercury is only slightly larger than Callisto, but Mercury is much more massive. That is because Callisto is made of much lighter and much less densely packed material. Callisto consists of about 40 percent ice and about 60 percent iron rock. Unlike Ganymede, the mixture of materials within Callisto seems to be uniformly distributed.

Callisto is a "dead moon." It offers an archive of ancient solar system history that has been preserved for billions of years, but scientists doubt that any form of life ever brightened this dark, cold, isolated place.

Callisto has the oldest and most heavily cratered surface in the solar system.

## A Dozen Dumplings

The rest of Jupiter's moons are smaller and more irregularly shaped than the Galilean moons. They look like odd-sized dumplings hovering around Jupiter's giant glow. Four of these moons are closer to Jupiter than the Galilean moons. The other eight are more distant.

Several of these moons were discovered by the two Voyager spacecraft. *Voyager 1* also sent back images of something even more

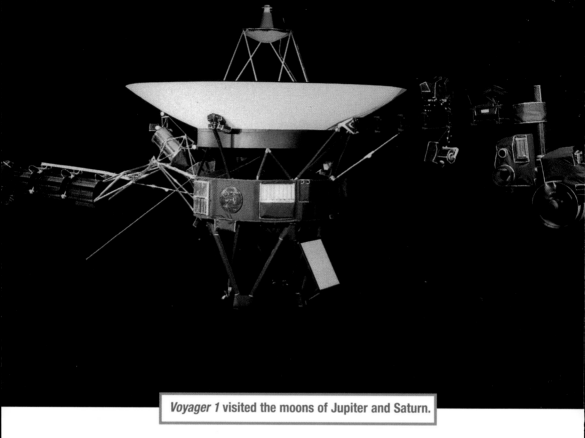

*Voyager 1* **visited the moons of Jupiter and Saturn.**

surprising—a thin ring around the mighty planet. Scientists have known about Saturn's rings for more than 300 years, but this was the first evidence that other gas giants have rings. Jupiter's rings are difficult to see because they are made of very small, dark particles of dust and rock. Unlike Saturn's rings, Jupiter's rings do not appear to contain any ice.

In 1998, *Galileo* provided information that allowed scientists to identify four separate rings—an inner cloud-like ring called a halo;

a large, flat main ring; and two very faint gossamer rings. Data collected by the spacecraft also helped scientists figure out how the rings formed.

Each of the rings consists of dust hurled into space when meteoroids struck one of Jupiter's small inner moons. The halo is made up of debris that was once part of Metis, Jupiter's innermost moon. Similarly, the main ring formed from particles that were once part of the tiny moon Adrastea. The two gossamer rings are made up of material from Amalthea and Thebe. Amalthea has the distinction of being the reddest object in the solar system. Its unusual color may come from sulfur cast off by nearby Io.

Jupiter's other eight known moons range in size from 9 to 115 miles (15 to 185 km) across. They fall into two groups—the inner four and the outer four. The inner four—Leda, Himalia, Lysithea and Elara—orbit about 7 million miles (11 million km) from Jupiter. The outer four—Ananke, Carme, Pasiphae, and Sinope—are much farther out. Ananke is more than 13 million miles (21 million km) from Jupiter. The others are at least 14 million miles (23 million km) away.

Although most of Jupiter's moons travel clockwise as they circle the king of the planets, Ananke, Carme, Pasiphae, and Sinope move counterclockwise. It is unusual for moons to move against the spin of the planet they orbit, so scientists believe the outer moons were once asteroids. At some point, they were captured by Jupiter's powerful gravity.

With these small, distant moons, your journey through the mysterious Jupiter system ends. Moving farther outward—toward the magnificent beauty of Saturn and its moons—many other wonders lie ahead.

# Chapter 4

# The Family of Saturn

F ar in the distance, Saturn's pale glow beckons. The splendid beauty of the huge, butterscotch-colored planet and its magnificent rings has long attracted scientists and poets. But there is more to the Saturn system than the planet and its rings. The family of Saturn includes eighteen named moons, and as many as twelve others have been sighted in recent years. These moons have not been named because scientists do not yet know enough about them and their orbital paths to be sure that they are all separate moons.

The first thirteen moons were discovered by scientists using telescopes. Many were spotted at a specific point in Saturn's orbit. Every 15 years or so, Saturn's rings are turned on edge in relation to Earth. As a result, the rings nearly disappear from view. At these times, when the brightly glowing rings do not dominate our view of Saturn, scientists are able to get a better glimpse of the planet's moons.

No planet in the solar system has more moons than Saturn, and each one has a colorful history. Most of Saturn's moons are small and rocky. Some are so close to the planet that they influence the planet's rings. Others are lonely and silent, far from the rush and the hubbub.

## Titan: Another Possible Cradle of Life?

The largest and most important of Saturn's many moons is an icy sphere surrounded by a thick, murky, smoglike atmosphere. This faraway world is known as Titan.

For a moon, Titan is, well, titanic. It has a diameter of 3,200 miles (5,150 km). Titan is larger than two of the solar system's nine planets, outstripping both Mercury and Pluto in size. It is the second largest of all the known moons. Only Jupiter's moon Ganymede is larger. And if you count its atmosphere, Titan outmeasures even Ganymede. In fact, Titan is nearly as large as Mars!

For many years, scientists didn't know much about Titan because a deep layer of clouds in its upper atmosphere forms an orange-brown haze around it. When *Pioneer 11* flew by in 1979, the images it took showed nothing more than a fuzzy ball. Photos taken by *Voyager 1* in 1980 weren't much better. Scientists say that Titan's haze is similar to the smog in Los Angeles, California. In fact, Titan is the smoggiest sphere in the solar system.

*Voyager 1* captured this image of Titan in 1980. At the time, some people described the moon as an orange in the sky.

In 1993, the Hubble Space Telescope let scientists see what lies below the smog. Titan's surface has one bright area about as big as Australia and several large dark patches. Although these images only hinted at what Titan's surface is like, the bright area could be a mountain of frozen water and ammonia ice. The dark patches may be lakes or small oceans of ethane or *methane* gas.

Although scientists have spent many hours studying the orange moon, they are still not sure how its atmosphere formed or why it has not lost its thick, gassy clouds over time. Is the atmosphere composed of primordial gases that date back to the beginning of the big moon's creation? Were they trapped in its icy surface and released slowly over the ages? Scientists hope to answer these questions someday soon.

## A Bird and a Parachute: Mission to Titan

On October 15, 1997, NASA launched a space probe called *Cassini/Huygens* from Kennedy Space Center on Cape Canaveral in Florida. The spacecraft is scheduled to reach Saturn in July 2004, and will spend at least 4 years orbiting and studying the planet, its rings, and its moons. One of the *Cassini Saturn Orbiter*'s goals is to create a detailed map of Titan's surface.

In November 2004, the *Huygens Titan Probe* will separate from the main spacecraft and drop into Titan's thick atmosphere. The probe, which was built by the European Space Agency—a group of space scientists funded by several Western European nations—has three parachutes and a heatshield to protect it.

*Cassini/Huygens* as it may look travelling through the solar system to visit Saturn's largest moon, Titan.

Besides showing us exactly what's beneath the giant moon's orange haze, the *Huygens Probe* will collect and analyze samples of the chemicals in its atmosphere. A microphone on board the probe will detect any noises coming from the moon's surface. These might include the sounds of wind blowing, thunder clapping, rocks cracking, or ice crunching.

**Christiaan Huygens**

The Dutch scientist Christiaan Huygens (1629–1695) had many talents. Even as a boy he had an obvious knack for math and mechanics. His father liked to call him "my Archimedes," after the famous ancient Greek mathematician. Private teachers had Christiaan ready for college by age 16. He studied law and mathematics at the University of Leiden and later at the College of Orange at Breda. Christiaan spoke fluent French and English (in addition to his native Dutch), and he excelled in music. He was a card and billiard shark, and he rode horses masterfully. He was popular with women, although he never married.

Huygens made his mark in many fields, including probability and gambling, music, optics, and physics. He is known for his wave theory of light, and he also patented the first pendulum clock.

For astronomers, Huygens invented a telescope eyepiece. It was a big improvement, and using one of these lenses, he was the first person to observe Saturn's big moon Titan in 1655. He was also the first to see that what Galileo described as the "tripleness" of Saturn actually was a separate ring around the planet.

Researchers suspect that Titan's atmosphere may be very similar to the atmosphere on Earth millions, or even billions, of years ago. If they are right, it is possible that primitive life forms might be developing on Titan right now.

If so, they would be struggling against terrible cold. Temperatures as low as −289°F (−178°C) are not unusual. Titan is located 759,200 miles (1,221,850 km) away from the warmth of Saturn's center. The cold does not necessarily rule out the possible existence of life on Titan, however. Although it seems unlikely that liquid water exists on Titan, liquid nitrogen could be present. Methane could exist as a solid, liquid, and a gas at such low temperatures. Perhaps some type of rainfall and liquid oceans could exist on Titan. If so, perhaps the materials on Titan could play the same role as water on Earth.

According to planetary scientist Don Miller, Titan's surface might have craggy, rock-lined shores and tidepools of murky, orange liquid that reflects the sky's dense, orangish haze. Another scientist envisions the moon's surface as a vast swampland dotted with pools of liquid nitrogen that teem with *hydrocarbon* goo. Both nitrogen and hydrocarbons are key ingredients for life.

Although Titan is probably too cold to support life as we know it, the big moon's similarities to primitive Earth are startling. Titan has an atmosphere composed primarily of nitrogen and a wide variety of organic molecules. The moon may have ocean and land areas.

Four or five billion years from now, our Sun will have matured into a *red giant*. At this stage, it will turn red and begin to swell tremendously. Mercury and Venus will burn up and disappear into the expanding Sun, and the oceans of Earth will boil away. The Sun's heat will reach farther and farther out into the solar system. Eventually, Titan may become warm enough for life to develop and evolve. Then, long after human life on Earth is gone, life may thrive on the orange moon that orbits the great ringed planet.

## The Nearby Moons

While Saturn's other moons hold no promise of supporting life, they too are interesting. The moons closest to Saturn dance nimbly among its rings. Three of Saturn's innermost moons—Atlas, Prometheus, and Pandora—are called *shepherd moons*. Like a shepherd who herds a flock of animals, shepherd moons use their gravitational attraction to keep the particles in Saturn's rings together.

Farther out, two small irregular moons play leapfrog 94,000 miles (151,000 km) above Saturn's clouds. Epimetheus and Janus are nearly

the same size, low in density, and icy. Strangely, they share nearly the same orbit. But just as they seem about to collide, one quickly moves out of the other's way.

All the moons that skip through and around Saturn's rings are in constant danger of being struck by meteoroids pulled toward Saturn by gravity. That is why scientists think that these moons may not be very old. Perhaps they are ever-changing fragments—split apart by impacts and then re-formed by gravitational attraction.

## Mimas: A Bulging Eyeball

The rest of Saturn's moons are found outside of its rings. The closest of these is Mimas, which looks more like a bulging eyeball than a moon. Mimas orbits only 115,280 miles (185,520 km) from Saturn. Although it is only about one-tenth as big as Earth's Moon, Mimas is one of Saturn's larger spherical moons.

Meteoroids and asteroids have heavily pummeled the surface of Mimas. Its pitted surface is twelve times more scarred than Saturn's outer moons. In fact, a giant crater covering much of the moon's face gives it the eyeball effect. This cavity, called Herschel crater, measures 80 miles (130 km) across—one-third of Mimas's diameter. Some parts of Herschel's outer edge are 32,800 feet (1,000 m) high. A mountain at its center towers 13,000 feet (4,000 m) high, nearly half as high as Earth's Mount Everest.

Some scientists think that this little moon may once have been part of a larger moon. The original moon may have been blown to pieces by

Herschel crater (upper right) on Mimas is equal to one-third the moon's diameter.

a meteoroid zooming toward Saturn. Later, some of the pieces may have reassembled into a jumbled mass held together by gravity. Such an explosion could be responsible for some of the fragments found close to Mimas. It is also possible that some material from the larger moon is now found in Saturn's rings.

## Enceladus: The Moon with the Makeover

Enceladus orbits 147,900 miles (238,020 km) from Saturn's center—about the same distance as our Moon is from Earth. Enceladus is much smaller than the Moon, however. It measures only 311 miles (500 km) across. Enceladus could easily fit inside the state of Texas.

Of all the moons in Saturn's system, Enceladus has the youngest face and shows the most geological activity. Like its neighbors farther out—Rhea, Dione, and Tethys—Enceladus seems to be made mostly of frozen water. However, it looks quite different. Its three neighbors all have heavily pockmarked surfaces—surfaces that have not changed in a long, long time. Because the surface of Enceladus reflects almost 100 percent of the sunlight that strikes it, the moon looks like a glowing ball.

Enceladus has some cratered areas, but it also has broad, smooth plains almost completely unmarked by cratering. Why is Enceladus so different? Why isn't this moon just another pockmarked iceberg? Some process has covered over the impact craters that must have once covered its surface. Something has flattened the cracks and ridges into smooth, featureless plains. The face of Enceladus has had a makeover. But how? And why?

The dark lines on Enceladus's surface look like sporadic marks made by a giant felt-tipped pen. These signs of surface cracking and

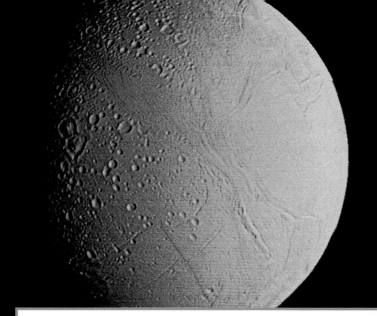

Enceladus's smooth surface, with its tiny, shallow pockmarks, is an unusual moon. Most moons in our solar system are heavily cratered.

fracturing indicate that much of the little moon's cratering has eroded. The surface may have melted away and then refrozen, or it may have flooded with fluids that later formed its smooth, icy crust. The few craters that are visible on the surface must have formed relatively recently—sometime in the last several hundred million years.

For melting or flooding to occur on Enceladus, there must have been a source of heat. Where did that heat come from? Could tidal forces, similar to those affecting Jupiter's moon Io be responsible? Probably not, according to planetary scientists. Calculations indicate that tidal forces in the Saturn system are probably not strong enough to do the job, so the mystery remains.

## The Three "Typical" Moons

Tethys, Dione, and Rhea are model moons. They closely resemble the type of moons scientists originally expected to find throughout the solar system. They are covered with frozen water and marked by layer on layer of craters. Many of the craters probably date back to the formation of the solar system. These bright moons have dark patches that are probably dirt. The craters are draped with bright material that is probably frost.

Tethys's orbit is just 36,000 miles (57,936 km) from Enceladus's. Tethys is about one-third the size of Earth's moon and has an icy crust marked with enormous cracks. One huge crack, the Ithaca Chasma, covers 75 percent of the moon's circumference. It is long enough to stretch nearly all the way from San Francisco to Los Angeles. Scientists speculate that Tethys was once made of fluid, but soon developed a hard crust. Whenever the fluid interior shifted, the moon's crust cracked.

Tethys plays a strange game of tag with two other moons—Telesto and Calypso. Researchers discovered these two small, irregular moons as they looked through Voyager photos in 1981. To everyone's surprise, they travel in the same orbit—on either side of Tethys!

Dione and Tethys are considered sister moons. Dione is a little larger, but quite a bit denser than Tethys. Scientists believe that Dione consists of a rocky core covered with a thick layer of frozen water.

Scientists think of Tethys (below) and Dione (right) as sister moons. Tethys is about one-third the size of Earth's Moon. Dione is a little larger and more heavily cratered.

Like our Moon, Dione always leads with the same hemisphere as it travels around Saturn. Oddly, though, most of Dione's craters appear on the other side of the moon. This surprised scientists. Just as you would expect more insects to crash into a car's front windshield than its rear window, scientists expected more debris to strike the leading side of Dione. Some scientists suspect that, at one time, Dione led with its cratered hemisphere and that a very powerful impact spun the moon around.

In 1980, two astronomers using a ground-based telescope discovered something unexpected close to Dione—a tiny moon traveling a little ahead of its larger companion. Named Helene, this moon is irregularly shaped and only 20 miles (32 km) across.

Rhea is larger than Saturn's other two "typical" moons, and about half the size of Earth's Moon. It has been repeatedly bombarded over the last 4.5 billion years, so the surface of this moon has craters on top of craters. Apparently, no interior activity has ever brought new "skin" to the surface. Rhea's low density suggests that it contains no rock. Rhea is really a big snowball!

This view of Rhea is composed of three images taken by *Voyager 1* as it flew by Saturn's family of moons.

# Major Moons of Saturn

## Vital Statistics

| Moon | Diameter | Distance from Center of Saturn | Surface Composition | Discovery |
|------|----------|-------------------------------|---------------------|-----------|
| JANUS | 137 miles (220 km) | 94,120 miles (151,470 km) | Possibly mostly frozen water | 1966, confirmed in 1980 |
| MIMAS | 243 miles (392 km) | 115,280 miles (185,520 km) | Mostly frozen water | 1789 |
| ENCELADUS | 311 miles (500 km) | 147,900 miles (238,020 km) | Mostly frozen water | 1789 |
| TETHYS | 653 miles (1050 km) | 183,000 miles (294,660 km) | Mostly frozen water | 1684 |
| DIONE | 696 miles (1,120 km) | 234,500 miles (377,400 km) | Mostly frozen water | 1684 |
| RHEA | 951 miles (1,530 km) | 327,500 miles (527,040 km) | Mostly frozen water | 1672 |
| TITAN | 3,200 miles (5,150 km) | 759,200 miles (1,221,850 km) | Ices; liquid nitrogen and methane | 1655 |
| HYPERION | 255 miles (410 km) | 921,500 miles (1,484,000 km) | Possibly ices | 1848 |
| IAPETUS | 894 miles (1,440 km) | 2,212,000 miles (3,562,000 km) | Ice and rock | 1671 |
| PHOEBE | 137 miles (220 km) | 8,048,000 miles (12,952,000 km) | Carbonaceous soil | 1898 |

This artistic composite image shows Saturn and six of its largest moons—Mimas, Enceladus, Tethys, Dione, Rhea, and Titan—with Hyperion's surface sketched in the foreground. For artistic effect, color, scale, and orbits are not shown realistically.

## Hyperion: A Great Irregularity

On the other side of Titan, roams Hyperion—the largest non-spherical moon in the solar system. It tumbles weirdly through its strangely flattened, *eccentric orbit* nearly 922,000 miles (1.5 million km) from Saturn. Deep craters and chasms gouge the surface of this moon. The largest crater on Hyperion is 75 miles (120 km) across and 6.2 miles (10 km) deep.

Hyperion is made of low-density, icy material, but it looks something like a dark-red, overgrown squash. Some scientists think that a major collision blew part of Hyperion away long ago, leaving only this odd remnant behind.

## Iapetus: Half and Half

In a contest for oddity, though, the moon Iapetus may beat Hyperion. In some ways, Iapetus is like other moons. Like Rhea, Iapetus has a fixed leading side and a trailing side. And although it is spherical like most of Saturn's other moons, the strange thing is it has two distinct halves. One part of Iapetus is white, shiny, and bright, while the other half is a dark rusty-red color. The border between the two regions is uneven and curved.

Scientists believe that the bright portion of Iapetus is made of ice, and the darker area is made of dust or rock. It is possible that the reddish material may be debris shed by Phoebe, another of Saturn's moons. Or it may have oozed to the surface from deep inside the moon. Iapetus might even consist of organic materials similar to the complex hydrocarbon substances found on some ancient meteorites.

## Phoebe: Captured Asteroid?

Phoebe, Saturn's outermost moon, is located nearly 8 million miles (13 million km) from the ringed planet. Because this little moon is so far from Saturn, it takes 550 Earth-days to complete one orbit. Like the outer four moons of Jupiter, Phoebe travels counterclockwise. It also orbits in a different plane than Saturn's rings and most of the beautiful planet's other moons. Unlike Earth's Moon, Phoebe shows more than one face to Saturn. It rotates on its axis once every 9 hours.

When *Voyager 2* flew by Phoebe, it discovered that this moon is roughly spherical and reflects about 6 percent of the sunlight that hits it. Phoebe's dark-red color reminds scientists of a class of ancient asteroids with an abundance of organic compounds.

Could Phoebe be an asteroid masquerading as a moon? Was it captured by Saturn's powerful gravity as it whizzed through the solar system? Many scientists would answer these questions with a "yes." After all, Phoebe is much farther out than Saturn's other moons, it orbits in a different plane and in the opposite direction, and it is a different color than the other moons—a color like that of many asteroids. So Phoebe joins several other moons we have seen—Mars's Deimos and Phobos and Jupiter's outer four moons—as another possible asteroid posing as a moon.

## Outward Bound

Now, as you leave the Saturn system, you head beyond the realm of the great ringed planet to its more distant neighbors. There you'll encounter the strangely tilted system of Uranus and the satellite family of Neptune, the beautiful sapphire world named after the classical god of the seas.

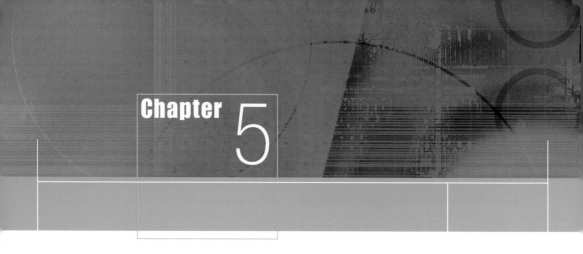

# Chapter 5

# The Moons of Uranus and Neptune

**B**efore the Voyager spacecraft sent back photos and collected data about the gas giants, most scientists thought Uranus and Neptune were very similar. After all, they are both composed primarily of gases, they are both blue, they are about the same size, and each has a bunch of moons. As far as scientists knew, Uranus had five moons and Neptune had two.

As it turned out, both worlds are more complex than scientists expected. We have now identified eighteen moons and a strange, system of thin rings swirling around Uranus. Neptune has a violently stormy atmosphere and highly active weather patterns. Eight moons and a thin, delicate ring orbit the giant planet.

The Voyager spacecraft taught us volumes about our solar system. Perhaps their greatest lesson was this: When it comes to the planets and their moons, expect the unexpected.

## At Uranus: Moons "Over Easy"

Uranus is a big, blue, featureless planet. It has no visible mountains or plains, no storm systems, and no swirling clouds. The strangest thing about Uranus is the way it orbits the Sun. Uranus's axis is tilted—a lot. Instead of being nearly upright like the other planets in our solar system, Uranus seems to be lying on its side. Despite the planet's unusual position, all its moons orbit around Uranus's equator.

No one knows exactly why Uranus is tipped over. Perhaps a huge mass of material hit Uranus as it was forming. The impact must not have been powerful enough to break Uranus apart, but great enough to tip the planet on its side. Ever since that time, Uranus has been orbiting the Sun in this cockeyed position.

Recently, many planetologists have become very interested in the role of giant impacts during the solar system's early formation. They have discovered that an object's rate of rotation and direction of spin can help them piece together what happened long ago. Many scientists can't wait to uncover the details of the story Uranus has to tell.

Before 1986, when *Voyager 2* flew through the Uranus system, we knew about only five of the planet's moons—Miranda, Ariel, Umbriel, Titania, and Oberon. Ariel, Umbriel, Titania, and Oberon are all about one-third to one-half the size of our Moon. All were first sighted from telescopes on Earth.

To our amazement, *Voyager 2* discovered ten new moons around Uranus. Most of them are small—less than 62 miles (100 km) in diameter. All these moons orbit between 31,050 and 362,000 miles (50,000 and 583,000 km) from the planet. Each of these moons circles the equator of the big, blue planet tipped on its side.

## Miranda:
## A Geological Treasure Trove

Of all the moons of Uranus, Miranda is the most intriguing. Some scientists call Miranda a "reassembled" moon. Others refer to it as a "jigsaw-puzzle world." This little patchwork moon is 301 miles (485 km) in diameter. It takes only about 1.5 days to complete its trip around Uranus. Tiny as Miranda is, it seems like many worlds in one—a sort of "cosmic geology museum."

Most of Miranda's jumbled crust is covered with old terrain, dotted with craters and rolling hills. Huge cracks cut across its surface, and land shifts have created cliffs that are six to nine times as deep as the Grand Canyon. Several dark regions surround oddly shaped brighter regions, including one bright area shaped like a giant 7.

How did this hodgepodge world form? Perhaps it was hit by an asteroid or another small moon moving fast enough to break Miranda into pieces. The pieces didn't travel far, though, and gravity soon drew them back together again. They reassembled in a jumble—inside out and backward. The resulting hodgepodge may even have absorbed the hurtling object that did all the damage. As a result, Miranda looks like a patchwork quilt, with geology and terrain of different ages stitched together by gravity and time.

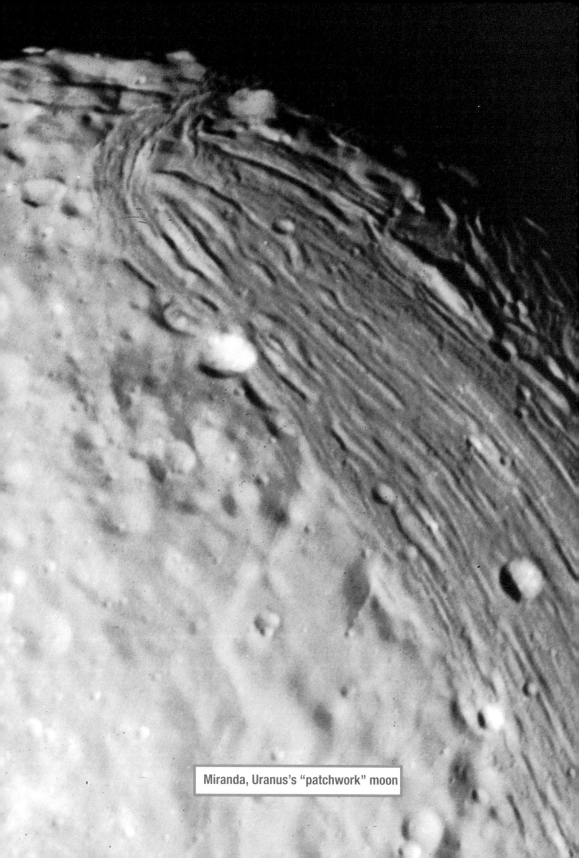

Miranda, Uranus's "patchwork" moon

Ariel (upper right) has a young, complex surface. Umbriel (center) has a bland, gray surface typical of the large moons of Uranus. Scientists think the light and dark areas in this *Voyager 2* image of Titania (lower right) may be associated with impact craters.

## The Other Four Large Moons

Uranus's largest moons seem to come in pairs. Ariel and Umbriel are both close to 700 miles (1,130 km) across. Ariel has a young, complex surface marked by wide, curving valleys and canyons. Its neighbor Umbriel has a recently blackened surface.

Titania is the largest moon in the Uranus system, with a diameter of 1,000 miles (1,610 km). Oberon is slightly smaller. Titania has

## A Brother-Sister Astronomy Team

William Herschel (1738–1822) and his sister Caroline Herschel (1750–1848) were working partners. Both started out as musicians—William was an organist and Caroline sang. Both also loved astronomy, though.

Late into the nights, in the freezing cold, they searched the skies through a huge home-built telescope. The two self-taught astronomers were fanatics about grinding and polishing the big lenses for their telescopes. They became the best telescope makers around. William's discovery of Uranus (1781) was just one of his many breakthroughs. Six years later he also spotted two of the planet's moons—Titania and Oberon (1787).

William's work is better known, but after her brother died in 1822, Caroline produced a catalog of 2,500 *nebulae*. For this work she received the Royal Astronomical Society's gold medal in 1828. Caroline lived to be nearly 98, and according to some accounts, she continued to "boogie into the night" with her sky watching and her music, well into her later years. The C Herschel crater on Earth's Moon is named in Caroline's honor.

William Herschel looks through the telescope that he and his sister, Caroline, built.

surface tracks that resemble the "string of pearls" on Jupiter's moon, Ganymede. These craters are probably the result of comet impacts that date back 3 to 4 billion years. Light, spraylike patterns on this moon suggest that material has spewed from within Titania and then fallen back to the surface where it froze.

Oberon, like Miranda, has high mountains and enormous faults. Deep valleys suggest that the crust once expanded and fractured, and was then filled in by materials that came from within the planet. Oberon's deep craters also show signs of flooding with some dark fluid and then freezing.

# The Larger Moons of Uranus

## Vital Statistics

| Moon | Diameter | Distance from Uranus | Surface Composition | Discovery |
|------|----------|----------------------|---------------------|-----------|
| MIRANDA | 301 miles (485 km) | 80,640 miles (129,780 km) | Frozen water and rock | 1948 |
| ARIEL | 721 miles (1,160 km) | 118,800 miles (191,240 km) | Frozen water and rock | 1851 |
| UMBRIEL | 739 miles (1,190 km) | 165,300 miles (265,970 km) | Frozen water and rock | 1851 |
| TITANIA | 1,000 miles (1,610 km) | 270,800 miles (435,840 km) | Frozen water and rock | 1787 |
| OBERON | 963 miles (1,550 km) | 362,000 miles 582,600 km) | Frozen water and rock | 1787 |

It's a tradition to name planets after characters in Roman myths.

When a moon is discovered, it is given a number until the International Astronomical Union assigns it an official name. The names of a planet's moons usually follow a theme. For example, Uranus's moons are the names of characters from plays written by William Shakespeare. Because Neptune is the god of the seas, its moons are named after characters described in Roman and Greek myths about the sea.

| Planet | Role of the God |
| --- | --- |
| MERCURY | Messenger of the gods |
| VENUS | Goddess of love |
| MARS | God of war |
| JUPITER | King of the gods |
| SATURN | God of planting and harvest |
| URANUS | Grandfather of all the gods; father of time |
| NEPTUNE | God of the seas |
| PLUTO | God of the underworld |

## Two "New" Moons Rising

In 1997, as four astronomers were examining the night sky with the Hale telescope in Palomar Mountain, California, they made an exciting discovery. They spotted two previously unidentified moons around Uranus. Although one discoverer hoped to name one of the moons after his cat Squeaker, they have been tentatively named Caliban and Sycorax.

Caliban and Sycorax are the faintest satellites ever discovered without the aid of a spacecraft. Both are irregularly shaped and follow eccentric paths. One discoverer describes them as "enormous, irregular lumps of dark ice and gunk."

## Neptune's Small Family

Most of Neptune's moons are small and orbit fairly close to the planet. Naiad, Thalassa, Despina, Galatea, and Larissa are all less than 46,600 miles (75,000 km) from Neptune. According to one planetologist, it's

# The Larger Moons of Neptune

## Vital Statistics

| Moon | Diameter | Distance from Neptune | Surface Composition | Discovery |
|---|---|---|---|---|
| PROTEUS | 261 miles (420 km) | 73,100 miles (117,600 km) | Possibly dark soil and ice | 1989 |
| TRITON | 1,678 miles (2,700 km) | 220,500 miles (354,800 km) | Methane ice | 1846 |
| NEREID | 211 miles (340 km) | 3,426,000 miles (5,513,400 km) | Methane ice | 1949 |

no surprise that astronomers on Earth never noticed these irregularly shaped moons because "they're as dark as soot."

While Triton is about 220,500 miles (354,800 km) out, only Nereid is very far from Neptune. Nereid has the most eccentric orbit in the solar system. At times, it is 3.5 million miles (5.5 million km) away from Neptune.

## Triton: Neptune's Backward Flyer

*Voyager 2* sent images of all Neptune's known moons back to Earth, but it taught us most about Triton. Triton was discovered in 1846, not long after Neptune itself was first spotted. An astronomer named William Lassell was the first person to see Neptune's largest moon. With a diameter of 1,678 miles (2,700 km), Triton is more than three-fourths the size of Earth's Moon and just a little smaller than Jupiter's moon, Europa.

Triton is another dramatic example of the many strange and "off-beat" moons in the outer solar system. In fact, Triton appears to be marching to the beat of an entirely different drummer. First of all, it spins backward. This means that if you were on Triton, the Sun would rise in the west and set in the east. Triton also revolves around Neptune in an eccentric orbit that is opposite to the direction in which Neptune spins.

Triton's oddities don't end there. Unlike most moons, it has a thin atmosphere. It also has unusual terrain with few craters. Instead, Triton has a fractured surface with flat, frozen "ice lakes" and a nubbly exterior that looks like the skin of a cantaloupe. Vents on the surface of Triton erupt like geysers, sending dark smoke straight up until it reaches high-altitude winds. There the smoke forms long, horizontal streamers that look like jet trails.

Such unusual behaviors and features have led scientists to suggest that Triton was once a planet in its own right, but was somehow knocked or pulled off its original course. Now it orbits Neptune.

No one is sure when Neptune captured Triton. Some scientists think it may have happened fairly recently. Did this event heat the moon's interior enough to produce the cantaloupe skin and the smoking vents we see now? Other researchers suggest that it happened billions of years ago, and that tidal forces from Neptune keep Triton hot the way Jupiter does Io. There might even be some other mysterious energy source at work deep within Triton. Perhaps scientists will have the answers they seek someday soon.

In 1998, the Hubble Space Telescope found evidence that Triton has heated up a lot since *Voyager 2* flew by. Researchers noticed that

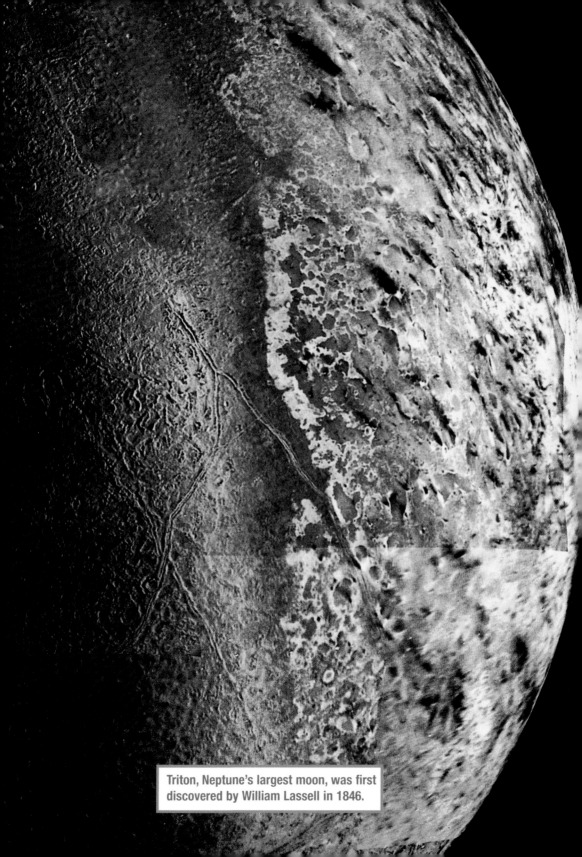

Triton, Neptune's largest moon, was first discovered by William Lassell in 1846.

the moon's atmosphere looks thicker. Has global warming turned some of the moon's frozen nitrogen to gas? These changes on Triton are somewhat similar to recent changes on our own planet.

Because Triton is a simpler world with a thin atmosphere, no oceans, and a surface of frozen nitrogen, studying this far-off world may help us to gain a better understanding of our own planet. Triton may also offer clues to the formation and history of the next places you will visit—Pluto and its moon Charon.

# Chapter 6

# Pluto and Charon: A Strange Duo

Far from the warmth and light of the Sun, the tiny world called Pluto travels the strangest path of all the planets. Pluto is so faint and distant that it completely escaped notice until 1930. That's when a young amateur astronomer named Clyde Tombaugh became the first person to spot it.

The little planet is only one-fifth the diameter of Earth, and it weighs 500 times less than Earth. By 1978, scientists realized that Pluto wasn't traveling alone. It has a moon, which we now know as Charon.

Like Uranus, Pluto is tipped on its side. And like Uranus's moons, Charon circles Pluto's equator as the two orbit the Sun in a long, eccentric orbit. Along the way, their paths intertwine in a continuously spiraling tango. Pluto rotates on its axis once every 6.4 Earth-days. Since Charon revolves around Pluto once every 6.4 days, the two bodies always keep the same face pointed toward each other. Astronomers call this arrangement a "locked synchronous rotation" because the two are synchronized, like two dancers moving to the same beat.

At one point in this orbit, Pluto and Charon come relatively close to the Sun. Most people think of Pluto as the outermost planet, but that's only true sometimes. During Pluto's summer season, it is closer to the Sun than Neptune is. The planet's icy surface vaporizes, and a thin, cold atmosphere of methane develops around it. Pluto last reached the point of its orbit closest to the Sun in 1989. Since a Pluto-year is equal to about 248 Earth-years, each season on Pluto lasts a very long time. In fact, its summer won't end until 2020.

## How Science Works: Observation at a Distance

In 1978, as James Christy of the U.S. Naval Observatory was studying some photographic images of Pluto, he noticed a lump on the side of the little planet. Had someone moved the telescope at the moment the image was captured? Christy looked at the stars in the image. They looked perfectly clear, so the telescope must have held steady.

Over the next few days, Christy saw that the lump traveled to the other side of Pluto. He realized the lump must be a moon. Christy had discovered Pluto's companion, Charon.

It is difficult to get a good view of Charon from Earth. Viewed through our planet's atmosphere, Charon and Pluto seem to blend into one lumpy blur. In 1996, the Hubble Space Telescope's Faint Object Camera took the only clear pictures we have of Pluto and Charon.

Scientists have also learned about the size and shape of the duo by using eclipses to their advantage. Whenever Charon blocks light from Pluto or Pluto blocks light from Charon, the pair looks dimmer. The larger the size of the disk that's blocking the light, the longer the dimness lasts. Although eclipses are usually rare, they occurred once every Pluto-day from 1985 to 1990.

An artist's view of Charon (center) and Pluto (top left)

The orbital path of Pluto takes the planet and its moon to the far edge of the solar system. From there, the Sun is a faraway, dim light.

In the middle of Pluto's winter, the planet is on the outer edges of the solar system. Just beyond lies a disk-shaped cloud called the Kuiper Belt. There, far from the Sun, scientists have detected objects left over from the formation of the solar system. In fact, some people call this region "a belt of orbiting rubble."

## Where Did Pluto and Charon Come From?

Because Pluto moves so close to the Kuiper Belt during its winter, some scientists think that it is not really a planet at all. They suggest that Pluto—and Charon—are jailbirds that somehow escaped from the Kuiper Belt. What evidence do they have? One important factor is Pluto's size. It is less than half the size of Mercury and smaller than seven of the moons in our solar system. It is only 2.5 times larger than Ceres, the largest-known asteroid.

Other scientists think Pluto may be an escaped moon of Neptune, rather than an object from the Kuiper Belt. They point to the fact that Pluto's composition is similar to Triton's—both have about the same mixture of ice and rock. These scientists have not proposed a theory to explain Charon's origin. Charon is not composed of the same materials as

# Pluto's Moon
## Vital Statistics

| Moon | Diameter | Distance from Pluto | Surface Composition | Discovery |
|------|----------|---------------------|---------------------|-----------|
| CHARON | 737 miles (1,186 km) | 12,054 miles (19,400 km) | Frozen water | 1978 |

Pluto and Triton. The surface of Charon is probably made of frozen water. Below the surface may be a rocky core. The moon may also contain frozen methane and nitrogen.

While scientists argue about Pluto's origin, no one can deny that it is unusual for such a small planet to have such a large moon. Charon is about 737 miles (1,186 km) in diameter—more than half the size of Pluto! Even Earth and its Moon are not that close in size. In fact, no other moon is as large compared to its planet as Charon. The two objects are just 12,054 miles (19,400 km) apart. Many people think of Pluto and Charon as a double-planet system—even stronger candidates for this classification than Earth and its Moon.

Someday, scientists may learn more about Pluto and Charon. NASA has already begun to plan a mission called the *Pluto-Kuiper Express*. The spacecraft will travel to the edge of the solar system and send back some close-up views of the mysterious duo.

The *Pluto-Kuiper Express* will visit Pluto, Charon, and the edge of the solar system.

With Pluto and Charon, our tour of the moons in our solar system comes to an end. This book has provided some basic information, but there is much more to learn. While you have been reading this book, space probes have been traveling to exciting destinations and others have been sending reams of data back to scientists on Earth.

Each week, newspapers all over the world carry stories of our newest space discoveries. In the future, scientists will undoubtedly learn more about moons and planets, our solar system, our galaxy, and the Universe. In the process, they will also learn more about our own Earth and how to preserve it for future generations.

Recently, scientists have begun to find solid evidence of planets orbiting other stars in the Universe. Could these planets have moons, too? Could some of these distant planets, or any moons that orbit them, support life? In the future, scientists will seek answers to our questions about the Universe not only from stars and planets, but also from the worlds around worlds within our solar system and beyond.

# Moons of the Solar System

## Vital Statistics

| Planet | Moon | Diameter | Distance from Center of Planet |
|--------|------|----------|-------------------------------|
| EARTH | Moon/Luna | 2,160 miles (3,476 km) | 238,860 miles (384,400 km) |
| MARS | Phobos | 17 miles (27 km) | 5,830 miles (9,380 km) |
| | Deimos | 9.3 miles (15 km) | 14,580 miles (23,460 km) |
| JUPITER | Metis | 25 miles (40 km) | 79,535 miles (128,000 km) |
| | Adrastea | 12 miles (20 km) | 80,157 miles (129,000 km) |
| | Amalthea | 163 miles (262 km) | 112,654 miles (181,300 km) |
| | Thebe | 62 miles (100 km) | 137,882 miles (221,900 km) |
| | Io | 2,259 miles (3,636 km) | 261,970 miles (421,600 km) |
| | Europa | 1,939 miles (3,120 km) | 416,900 miles (670,900 km) |
| | Ganymede | 3,273 miles (5,268 km) | 664,900 miles (1,070,000 km) |

| Planet | Moon | Diameter | Distance from Center of Planet |
|---|---|---|---|
| JUPITER (continued) | Callisto | 2,994 miles (4,818 km) | 1,170,000 miles (1,883,000 km) |
| | Leda | 6.2 miles (10 km) | 6,893,479 miles (11,094,000 km) |
| | Himalia | 106 miles (170 km) | 7,133,328 miles (11,480,000 km) |
| | Lysithea | 15 miles (24 km) | 7,282,456 miles (11,720,000 km) |
| | Elara | 50 miles (80 km) | 7,293,020 miles (11,737,000 km) |
| | Ananke | 12 miles (20 km) | 13,173,044 miles (21,200,000 km) |
| | Carme | 19 miles (30 km) | 14,042,962 miles (22,600,000 km) |
| | Pasiphae | 22 miles (36 km) | 14,602,195 miles (23,500,000 km) |
| | Sinope | 17 miles (28 km) | 14,726,469 miles (23,700,000 km) |
| SATURN | Pan | 12 miles (20 km) | 83,015 miles (133,600 km) |
| | Atlas | 24 miles (38 km) | 85,500 miles (137,600 km) |
| | Prometheus | 92 miles (148 km) | 86,557 miles (139,300 km) |
| | Pandora | 68 miles (110 km) | 88,048 miles (141,700 km) |
| | Epimetheus | 86 miles (138 km) | 94,075 miles (151,400 km) |
| | Janus | 137 miles (220 km) | 94,120 miles (151,470 km) |

| Planet | Moon | Diameter | Distance from Center of Planet |
|---|---|---|---|
| SATURN (continued) | Mimas | 243 miles (392 km) | 115,280 miles (185,520 km) |
| | Enceladus | 311 miles (500 km) | 147,900 miles (238,020 km) |
| | Tethys | 653 miles (1050 km) | 183,900 miles (295,960 km)* |
| | Calypso | 19 miles (30 km) | 183,900 miles (295,956 km)* |
| | Telesto | 19 miles (30 km) | 183,900 miles (295,960 km)* |
| | Dione | 696 miles (1,120 km) | 234,500 miles (377,400 km)† |
| | Helene | 20 miles (32 km) | 324,500 miles (377,400 km)† |
| | Rhea | 951 miles (1,530 km) | 327,500 miles (527,040 km) |
| | Titan | 3,200 miles (5,150 km) | 759,200 miles (1,221,850 km) |
| | Hyperion | 255 miles (410 km) | 921,500 miles (1,484,000 km) |
| | Iapetus | 894 miles (1,440 km) | 2,212,000 miles (3,562,000 km) |
| | Phoebe | 137 miles (220 km) | 8,048,000 miles (12,952,000 km) |
| URANUS | Cordelia | 16 miles (26 km) | 30,913 miles (49,750 km) |
| | Ophelia | 19 miles (30 km) | 33,405 miles (53,760 km) |
| | Bianca | 26 miles (42 km) | 36,760 miles (59,160 km) |

| Planet | Moon | Diameter | Distance from Center of Planet |
|---|---|---|---|
| URANUS continued | Cressida | 39 miles (62 km) | 38,388 miles (61,780 km) |
| | Desdemona | 34 miles (54 km) | 38,935 miles (62,660 km) |
| | Juliet | 52 miles (84 km) | 39,991 miles (64,360 km) |
| | Portia | 67 miles (108 km) | 41,073 miles (66,100 km) |
| | Rosalind | 34 miles (54 km) | 43,452 miles (69,930 km) |
| | Belinda | 41 miles (66 km) | 46,764 miles (75,260 km) |
| | Puck | 96 miles (154 km) | 53,438 miles (86,000 km) |
| | Miranda | 301 miles (485 km) | 80,640 miles (129,780 km) |
| | Ariel | 721 miles (1,160 km) | 118,800 miles (191,240 km) |
| | Umbriel | 739 miles (1,190 km) | 165,300 miles (265,970 km) |
| | Titania | 1,000 miles (1,610 km) | 270,800 miles (435,840 km) |
| | Oberon | 963 miles (1,550 km) | 362,000 miles (582,600 km) |
| | Satellite 1986 U10 | 25 miles (40 km) | 650,000 miles (1 million km) |
| | Caliban | 37 miles (60 km)‡ | 4,454,602 miles (7,169,000 km) |
| | Sycorax | 75 miles (120 km)‡ | 7,589,413 miles (12,214,000 km) |

| Planet | Moon | Diameter | Distance from Center of Planet |
|--------|------|----------|-------------------------------|
| NEPTUNE | Naiad | 36 miles (58 km) | 29,969 miles (48,230 km) |
| | Thalassa | 50 miles (80 km) | 31,118 miles (50,080 km) |
| | Despina | 92 miles (148 km) | 32,641 miles (52,530 km) |
| | Galatea | 98 miles (158 km) | 38,494 miles (61,950 km) |
| | Larissa | 129 mile (208 km) | 45,702 miles (73,550 km) |
| | Proteus | 261 miles (420 km) | 73,100 miles (117,600 km) |
| | Triton | 1,678 miles (2,700 km) | 220,500 miles (354,800 km) |
| | Nereid | 211 miles (340 km) | 3,426,000 miles (5,513,400 km) |
| PLUTO | Charon | 737 miles (1,186 km) | 12,054 miles (19,400 km) |

*Tethys, Calypso, and Telesto share the same orbit.
†Dione and Helene share the same orbit.
‡Approximate diameters.

# Exploring Moons: A Timeline

**1957** — The former Soviet Union, or USSR, launches the first artificial satellite, *Sputnik 1.*

**1958** — Launch of first U.S. satellite *Explorer 1.*

**1959** — The USSR's *Luna 1* probe to the Moon becomes the first spacecraft to leave Earth orbit.

**1959** — First images from the far side of the Moon are transmitted by *Luna 3.*

**1966** — First pictures from the surface of the Moon are sent back by *Luna 9.*

**1968** — During the Apollo 8 mission, three American astronauts become the first humans to circle the Moon.

**1969** — During the Apollo 11 mission, two American astronauts become the first human beings to walk on the Moon. More than 1 billion people worldwide watch the event live on television.

| | |
|---|---|
| **1970** | — During the Apollo 13 mission, technical problems force the three American astronauts on board to circle the Moon and return to Earth on reduced power. |
| **1970** | — *Lunokhod 1* rover becomes the first moving device on the Moon's surface. |
| **1971** | — *Mariner 9* sends back the first photos of the Martian moons Phobos and Deimos and maps most of the surface of Mars. |
| **1972** | — NASA launches *Apollo 17*, the last spacecraft to transport people to the Moon. |
| **1977** | — During its mission to Mars, *Viking 1 Orbiter* takes photos of Phobos. |
| **1979** | — *Pioneer 11* takes the first space-age look at Titan and the Saturn system. |
| **1979** | — *Voyager 1* and *Voyager 2* visit Jupiter and its moons and send back the first detailed images. |

| 1980 | — *Voyager 1* flies by Saturn and its moons. |
| 1981 | — *Voyager 2* flies by Saturn and its moons. |
| 1983 | — *Pioneer 10* leaves the solar system. |
| 1986 | — *Voyager 2* visits Uranus and its moons. |
| 1989 | — *Phobos 2* sends back a few images of Phobos before communication is lost. |
| 1989 | — *Galileo* is launched to Jupiter and the four Galilean moons. |
| 1994 | — *Galileo* flies by the asteroid Ida and photographs its moon Dactyl. It is the first asteroid known to have a moon. |
| 1995 | — Repaired Hubble Space Telescope provides first good close-up of Titan. |
| 1997 | — *Pathfinder* arrives at Mars. |
| 1997 | — *Cassini/Huygens* is launched and heads for Saturn and Titan. |

| | |
|---|---|
| **1995 – 98** | — *Galileo* drops a probe into the clouds of Jupiter and then makes an extended tour of the Galilean moons. |
| **1999** | — Using a ground-based telescope, astronomers in Colorado discover a moon orbiting the asteroid Eugenia. |
| **1999** | — Japan's *Mission Hope (Nozoni)* arrives at Mars and its moons. |
| **2000** | — *Cassini* flies by Jupiter. |
| **2004** | — *Cassini/Huygens* expected to arrive at Saturn and Titan. |

*asteroid*—a piece of rocky debris left over from the formation of the solar system 4.6 billion years ago. Most asteroids orbit the Sun in a belt between Mars and Jupiter.

*asteroid belt*—the region in space between Mars and Jupiter where most asteroids are found. It is 100 million miles (161 million km) wide.

*atmosphere*—the gases that surround a planet or other body in space.

*astronomical unit (AU)*—the mean distance of Earth from the Sun—1 AU = 93 million miles (150 million km). This measurement is often used to express distances within the solar system.

*axis*—the imaginary line running from pole to pole through the center of a planet or moon. A celestial body spins, or rotates, along its axis.

*comet*—a small ball of rock and ice that travels toward the Sun in a long orbit that originates on the remote outer edge of the solar system.

*composition*—the materials that make up an object, such as a moon or planet.

*core*—the innermost region of a moon or planet.

*crater*—an irregular circular or oval depression in the surface of a planet or moon made by a collision with another object.

*crust*—the outer surface of a moon or planet.

*density*—how much of a substance exists in a given volume.

*diameter*—the distance across the center of a circle or sphere.

*eccentric orbit*—an orbit that looks more like a flattened oval than a perfect circle.

*gas giant*—a very large planet composed mostly of gas. The four gas giants are Jupiter, Saturn, Uranus, and Neptune.

*gravitational field*—the area of space affected by a planet's gravity.

*gravity*—the force that pulls objects toward the center of a planet, moon, or other object in space. All objects have some gravity. The larger an object is, the more gravity it has.

*hydrocarbon*—a compound that consists of hydrogen and carbon atoms only; one of the key classes of organic compounds.

*hypothesis*—an assumption made in order to test a scientific idea.

*mantle*—a geologically unique region below the crust and above the core of a moon or planet.

*mass*—the amount of matter or material in an object.

*meteor*—the glowing light we see in the night sky when a meteoroid is in contact with Earth's atmosphere.

*meteorite*—a particle of dust or rock that hits another object, such as a moon or planet.

*meteoroid*—a rocky or metallic object of relatively small size, usually once part of a comet or asteroid.

*methane*—a hydrocarbon gas; one of the major ingredients of the atmosphere of Titan.

*nebula* (**pl.** *nebulae*)—a cloud of gas and dust that may develop into a solar system.

*orbit*—the curved path followed by one body going around another body in space.

*planetologist*—a scientist who studies planets, moons, and other objects in space.

**red giant**—a star that is cooling, but remains bright and luminous. A red giant has a large volume, low surface temperature, and a reddish color.

**regolith**—a layer of weathered rock and soil that overlays bedrock.

**revolve**—to move in a path, or orbit, around another object. Earth revolves around the Sun, making a complete trip in 1 year.

**rille**—a long, narrow trench or valley on the Moon.

**rotation**—the turning of a body on its axis. Earth makes one complete rotation in 24 hours.

**satellite**—any object that orbits another object in space. The Moon is a satellite of Earth, and Earth is a satellite of the Sun. Human-made satellites are called "artificial" to distinguish them from natural satellites, such as moons.

**shepherd moon**—a moon that influences the position or width of a planetary ring.

**terrestrial**—relating to Earth.

The news from space changes fast, so it's always a good idea to check the copyright date on books, CD-ROMs, and video tapes to make sure that you are getting up-to-date information. One good place to look for current information from NASA is U.S. government depository libraries. There are several in each state.

## Books

Campbell, Ann Jeanette. *Amazing Space: A Book of Answers for Kids.* New York: John Wiley & Sons, 1997.

Dickinson, Terence. *Other Worlds: A Beginner's Guide to Planets and Moons.* Willowdale, Ontario: Firefly Books, 1995.

Gustafson, John. *Planets, Moons and Meteors.* (The Young Stargazer's Guide to the Galaxy) New York: Julian Messner, 1992.

Hartmann, William K. and Don Miller. *The Grand Tour.* New York: Workman Publishing, 1993.

Mechler, Gary (Editor), Steven Kent, Dr. Croft, Melinda Hutson. *Planets and Their Moons.* (National Audubon Society Pocket Guides) New York: Alfred Knopf, 1995.

Spangenburg, Ray, and Diane Moser. *Exploring the Reaches of the Solar System.* (Space Exploration) New York: Facts On File, Inc., 1990.

Vogt, Gregory L. *The Solar System Facts and Exploration.* New York: Twenty-First Century Books, 1995.

## CD-ROM

*Beyond Planet Earth.* Discovery Channel School Multimedia. Discovery Channel School, P.O. Box 970, Oxon Hill, MD 20750-0970.

## Video Tapes

*Discover Magazine: Solar System.* Discovery Channel School, P.O. Box 970, Oxon Hill, MD 20750-0970.

*On Jupiter.* Discovery Channel School, P.O. Box 970, Oxon Hill, MD 20750-0970.

## Organizations and Online Sites

Many of the online sites listed below are NASA sites, with links to many other interesting sources of information about moons and planetary systems. You can also sign up to receive NASA news on many subjects via e-mail.

**Astronomical Society of the Pacific**
*http://www.aspsky.org/*
390 Ashton Avenue
San Francisco, CA 94112

### NASA Ask a Space Scientist
*http://image.gsfc.nasa.gov/poetry/ask/askmag.html#list*
Take a look at the Interactive Page where NASA scientists answer your questions about astronomy, space, and space missions. This site also has access to archives and fact sheets.

### NASA Newsroom
*http://www.nasa.gov/newsinfo/newsroom.html*
This site features NASA's latest press releases, status reports, and fact sheets. It includes a news archive with past reports and a search button for the NASA website. You can even sign up for e-mail versions of all NASA press releases.

### National Space Society
*http://www.nss.org*
600 Pennsylvania Avenue, S.E., Suite 201
Washington, DC 20003

### The Nine Planets: A Multimedia Tour of the Solar System
*http://www.seds.org/nineplanets/nineplanets/nineplanets.html*
This site has excellent material on moons. It was created and is maintained by the Students for the Exploration and Development of Space, University of Arizona.

### Planetary Missions
*http://nssdc.gsfc.nasa.gov/planetary/projects.html*
At this site, you'll find NASA links to current and past missions. It's a one-stop shopping center to a wealth of information.

**The Planetary Society**
*http://www.planetary.org/*
65 North Catalina Avenue
Pasadena, CA 91106-2301

**Project Galileo Home Page**
*http://www-a.jpl.nasa.gov/galileo/index.html*
This site features a section just for kids. Check out "What's Cool about Galileo?".

**Sky Online**
*http://www.skypub.com*
This is the website for *Sky and Telescope* magazine and other publications of Sky Publishing Corporation. You'll find a good weekly news section on general space and astronomy news. Of special interest are *Sky and Telescope* feature stories adapted especially for online reading. The site also has tips for amateur astronomers as well as a nice selection of links. A list of science museums, planetariums, and astronomy clubs organized by state can help you locate nearby places to visit.

### Welcome to the Planets

*http://pds.jpl.nasa.gov/planets/*

This tour of the solar system has lots of pictures and information. The site was created and is maintained by California Institute of Technology for NASA/Jet Propulsion Laboratory.

### Windows to the Universe

*http://windows.ivv.nasa.gov/*

This NASA site, developed by the University of Michigan, includes sections on "Our Planet," "Our Solar System," "Space Missions," and "Kids' Space." Choose from presentation levels of beginner, intermediate, or advanced. To begin exploring, go to the URL and choose "Enter the Site."

## Places to Visit

Check the Internet (*www.skypub*.com is a good place to start), your local visitor's center, or phone directory for planetariums and science museums near you. Here are a few suggestions.

### Exploratorium

3601 Lyon Street
San Francisco, CA 94123
*http://www.exploratorium.edu/*
You'll find internationally acclaimed interactive science exhibits, including astronomy subjects.

**Jet Propulsion Laboratory (JPL)**
4800 Oak Grove Drive
Pasadena, CA 91109
*http://www.jpl.nasa.gov/faq/#tour*
JPL is the primary mission center for all NASA planetary missions. Tours are available once or twice a week by arrangement.

**NASA Goddard Spaceflight Center**
Code 130, Public Affairs Office
Greenbelt, MD 20771
*http://pao.gsfc.nasa.gov/vc/info/info.htm*
Visitors can see a Moon rock brought back to Earth by Apollo astronauts as well as other related exhibits.

**National Air and Space Museum**
7th and Independence Ave., S.W.
Washington, DC 20560
*http://www.nasm.edu/NASMDOCS/VISIT/*
This museum, located on the National Mall west of the Capitol building, has all kinds of interesting exhibits.

**Space Center Houston**
Space Center Houston Information
1601 NASA Road 1
Houston, Texas 77058
*http://www.spacecenter.org/*
Space Center Houston offers a tour and exhibits related to humans in space, including the Apollo missions to the Moon.

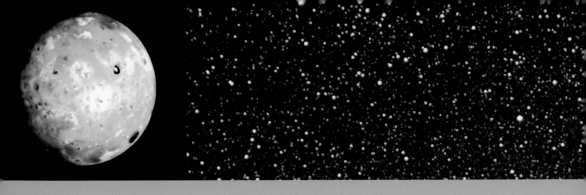

**Ray Spangenburg** and **Kit Moser** are a husband-and-wife writing team specializing in science and technology. They have written 33 books and more than 100 articles, including a five-book series on the history of science and a four-book series on the history of space exploration. As journalists, they covered NASA and related science activities for many years. They have flown on NASA's Kuiper Airborne Observatory, covered stories at the Deep Space Network in the Mojave Desert, and experienced zero-gravity on experimental NASA flights out of NASA Ames Research Center. They live in Carmichael, California, with their two dogs, Mencken (a Sharpei mix) and F. Scott Fitz (a Boston Terrier).